THE NEXT LEG OF MY JOURNEY

To your success.
with my favorite
Son ?

Len Chappell
6 - 16 - 2018

THE NEXT LEG OF MY JOURNEY

Lenor Madruga Chappell

iUniverse.com, Inc.
San Jose New York Lincoln Shanghai

The Next Leg of My Journey

Published by iUniverse.com, Inc.

For information address:
iUniverse.com, Inc.
5220 S 16th, Ste. 200
Lincoln, NE 68512
www.iuniverse.com

ISBN: 0-595-14639-2

Printed in the United States of America

Dedication

This book is dedicated to God for never letting me forget my "promessa."

To my daughters, Christianna and Daniella, for continuing to be "mommy's little legs."

To my husband, Roy, for his love and for the "adventure."

Epigraph

"To dream of the person you wish to be
is to waste the person you are."

.Author Unknown

Contents

Acknowledgements

I would like to give special thanks to the extraordinary people who were a part of this book:

Ernest Brawley, my brother, for his enthusiasm and his great edits.

Amy Belkin, Melinda Halderman, and Dianna Coogle, for encouraging me to write this sequel and investing their time and talent in editing the manuscript.

Doris Michaels, my agent, who hung in there to get this book published.

To Tiffany Adrever who's suggestions on revisions were invaluable.

To Diane Harris, my sister and best friend, who's my biggest fan.

To Nick del Pesco for the laughter and the memories.

Robbie Gordon, my buddy, for her cherished friendship.

Carlos Sambrano, my prosthetist, who keeps me on my "feet."

To Susan Silva, my assistant, computer wizard and friend.

Dana Isaacson at iUniverse who made *The Next Leg of My Journey* a reality.

Introduction

In 1974 I was living the American dream on a ranch outside a small town in northern California with my husband and two young daughters. I was a devoted wife and my husband a hardworking farmer of Portuguese descent. Joseph and I had been childhood sweethearts, and after ten years of marriage, we were still madly in love. And then catastrophe struck to the heart of our peaceful life.

On my 32nd birthday I discovered a hard lump on the left side of my groin. It turned out to be a malignant cartilage tumor, a rare form of bone cancer. The good news was that a cartilage tumor doesn't travel through the bloodstream as most tumors do. The bad news was that it was a notorious seeder, meaning that doctors could not risk dissecting the growth for fear it would spread to other areas of my body. The jarring reality was that I had only one option for cure: a hemi-pelvectomy—the amputation of my entire left leg and part of my pelvis. Without thinking of the consequences, I made my decision. I could accept the loss of my left leg, but I didn't want to die.

A successful surgery was performed at the Mayo Clinic. I was cured. It was over. But the terror had only just begun. For two days I lay in a semi-coma. I came to for moments at a time, but not long enough to remember where I was or what had happened. On the third day, I began to regain consciousness. I started to focus on faces as they came and went. I watched the nurses and felt their constant probing. And I recognized my husband at my side. I had made it through, and Joseph, my best friend, was my reassurance in this, my darkest hour. He held my hand as the hours of that long day passed slowly, and I gained strength by his tender and constant attention. I would be okay.

Late that night, alone, I got up the nerve to glance down to my left side. My heart stopped as my eyes met the flat of the sheet. I swallowed hard as I reached down. Then my hand, as if it had a life of its own, began to tap the sheet with quick, short jabs, moving higher and higher until it came to an abrupt end. "Oh, my God," I gasped. I had no idea the surgery would be so radical and unforgiving. Not only was my leg gone but half of my pelvis was missing. My silhouette was frightening, a stranger to me. I wept for my loss—for the wound that would never heal, and for the unfairness.

At first, I could do nothing but lose myself to the despair of this terrible human indignity. But it wasn't long before I realized I had to reclaim my life and summon the courage to fight back, not only for me but for my children and husband. It would be tough, the biggest challenge I had ever confronted. But I'd been given a gift—a second chance at life—and I couldn't throw it away.

During the next five years, I struggled with the many-headed beast of this disaster. I constantly feared the cancer would return. I had to endure the awful phantom limb pain that doctors had failed to mention, a torture so bizarre, so insistent and real, that I never actually felt the shock of losing my limb because my "missing leg" hurt too much. And I had to overcome my addiction to painkillers. Because I refused to accept doctors' words, "you will need a wheelchair; hemi-pelvectomies rarely ever walk," I had to cope with endless days, weeks and months of shopping for an artificial leg: I then had to accept the fact that I was forever dependent on a huge mechanical contraption that encased my hips and buttocks—an impostor that was now my left leg.

Like a child, I had to take my first steps. I understood all too soon that every step, every move would have to be carefully thought out. And even more disturbing, I had to face the hard fact that I would never again walk with ease or grace. My greatest fear, however, was anticipating that my new leg might collapse while I stepped off a curb or crossed a busy street. But just to walk to my husband and children, go to the store on my own, climb the two flights of stairs to our bedrooms, or mop the kitchen floor—all became extraordinary feats of pleasure for me and soon outweighed the impatience and difficulties of having to wear an artificial leg.

Those years were hard and consuming, but I got through them, *we* got through them. Joseph's and my relationship grew even stronger. My husband had never been more loving or attentive, and, to my relief, our frequent and passionate intimacy continued as before.

Joseph and I stood together as we always had with our girls, Christianna who was five years old and Daniella who was only two. We were a family. But the girls were baffled. "Where's your leg, mommy?" Christianna would continue to ask for a long time. "You left your leg somewhere. Please, mommy," she'd plead, "go back and get it."

Daniella remembers me only with one leg. "Let me cuddle in your empty spot, mommy," she would say.

Ultimately, with the love and support of my family and friends, I was able to get back on my feet and into a life that doctors thought impossible for a hemi-pelvectomy. I rode horses, water-skied, danced and continued to hostess local fashion shows.

And then my brother, novelist Ernest Brawley, came up with the idea for me to write my story. "Let me live it first," was my initial response.

But Ernie kept reminding me that there were people all over the world who cannot get beyond a devastating life experience because they succumb to a victim's mentality. They give up. Life stops. All they want is a glimmer of hope. All they need is to find a way out of their despair. "My God," Ernie persisted, " if there's a reason for anything, surely one of the reasons this happened to you is that you would find a way around every obstacle and care enough about life to spread the word to others not as strong as you."

Ernie was right. People needed to hear how one could triumph and overcome the odds, how I'd been able to return from the abyss of pain, drug addiction, and depression, and deal with all the negative things that threatened to control my life.

I also had an important reason of my own to write the story. The night before my amputation I had made a "promessa" (a Portuguese word, meaning a deeply held promise). "Please, God," I plea-bargained, "if you cure me of this cancer, I'll do anything—visit the sick, feed the poor, do church work, anything, if you grant me just one wish—my life."

When doctors gave me the final prognosis—a cure but only with radical amputation—I knew I had a pledge to keep. After returning home from the hospital, before I had fully healed, I volunteered at hospitals and rehabilitation centers. I accepted invitations to speak at churches, schools, civic and social clubs. I went anywhere I was invited. But was this enough? I exhausted myself in these endeavors, yet I couldn't let up. I had the uneasy superstition that God might back out of our pact if I did. I couldn't risk it.

So I took on my brother's proposition of writing my story. After four months I had written three chapters. I signed on with a New York agent who presented my proposal to a number of publishers, all of whom categorically rejected it.

"Why?" I asked my agent.

"The publishers returned your manuscript because they found it appalling," he said.

"Appalling," I cried out in confusion.

I knew I was disabled, partially disfigured, but I certainly didn't think I was "appalling." In the years since my illness, I had learned to accept the loss of my leg. I had also come to understand a simple truth: it's not so much what a person looks like, but what one projects that people respond to. This was the basic theme of my book, and I was determined to show these publishers that I was a woman who still considered herself feminine, attractive, and whole. I would go to New York and present to these publishers my own "far from appalling" self.

After meeting with three publishers, I was delighted to receive an offer from McGraw Hill.

One Step At A Time was published a year later. The moment it was released, my life changed forever. In a year I went from being a farm wife to a published author. It was the most exciting time of my life. I was living the best of both worlds—wife and mom, and career woman. After the publication of my book, I was immediately sent on national tours, my book was featured in major magazines, and Hollywood producers were offering options on attractive movie deals. It was heady stuff for me, but intimidating for Joseph. He muttered things about my book like, "flagrant intrusion of our privacy." Maybe it was partly that his Portuguese traditional view of the wife and mother was being challenged; maybe it was that my life was expanding into exciting new worlds while he felt stuck in an endless repetition of planting and harvesting.

It is true that up until the time I lost a leg and wrote a book, family, home and local activities had been my priorities. But now the need to answer the enormous amounts of mail from readers and to travel to promote my book became equal partners with my home responsibilities. Totally secure in my marriage, I had thought it safe to leave Joseph whenever I had to be away. And because Joseph never expressed any resentment toward me, I went about my merry way, rationalizing that I was having my "fifteen minutes of fame" and that our lives would settle down and get back to normal after the promotion of my book.

I was mistaken.

In 1981 I decided to go to France to try to sell my book, where it had been repeatedly rejected. Cancer meant death to most Europeans back then, thus books dealing with cancer were considered taboo at that time. I wanted to use my book to dispel the fears that cancer was a death sentence.

I asked Joseph if he would like to go with me, but he declined, saying he had too much work on the farm. So on a bright day in mid-summer, I kissed Joseph good-by at the San Francisco airport. Excited, I was totally unaware of any relief or animosity that might have been beneath Joseph's stoic exterior. He was taking care of the farm, and I was off to Paris to sell my book.

My second week in Paris the book was picked up by a French publisher.

When I returned home, everything seemed normal to me. Joseph was busy irrigating crops and the children were enjoying their last days of summer vacation. Shortly before Christmas, Joseph and I danced like lovers at our friend's annual party. While we danced, Joseph held me close, kissed me, and whispered that he loved me. I thought how happy and lucky I was on that Christmas holiday.

But two days later on Christmas day, all the love and happiness we had shared for so many years was shattered when I witnessed a wife's worst nightmare.

Chapter 1
Is This Christmas?

If you have to leave a place that you have lived in and loved, where all your yesterdays are buried deep, leave it the fastest way you can.

Beryl Markham, West With The Night

Dawn quietly broke on Christmas morning of 1981. I woke up on the couch.

I heard Joseph's truck zigzagging down the lane toward our old Victorian house. Hours before, after our daughters had unwrapped their Christmas Eve gifts, he had said he was going to town for cigarettes. Any excuse to leave in the evening had become a familiar and disturbing pattern over the past year.

The sleepless night on the couch had left me ragged and fatigued. How unfair, I thought. Joseph will sleep it off for half the day while I'll be left to get things ready for Christmas day pretending nothing had happened.

I didn't bother to put on my leg but made my way to the kitchen on crutches feeling angry at Joseph but relieved he was home safely. I loved this man—his touch, his smell, his powerful body, his handsome face. But I was irritated and frustrated that he had ruined another evening for his family.

Arms crossed in judgment, I posed before the kitchen sink in the wifely stance I had perfected over the last year. I heard his key slip quietly into the door and the familiar sound of his cowboy boots clicking across the back porch floor. When he entered, I knew he was hoping he'd gotten lucky and I'd be upstairs asleep. When he saw me, he staggered over and tried to explain.

"Don't bother, Joseph; I'm tired," I said in a dead voice. "I'm going to bed. I have to be up in an hour to get things ready for Christmas." I grabbed my crutches and went upstairs, with Joseph following close behind. I crawled into bed while he stood at the foot of the bed, red-eyed, swaying, trying to explain where he'd been all night. I found myself wondering why it was so important for him to reassure me that he'd been with the guys. It had never occurred to me he'd be anywhere else.

"Please, Lenor, believe me, I'm sorry. It won't happen again."

"All right, all right," I said, a little confused, but too exhausted to care. "I believe you. Now just go back to your friends, go wherever you want. Just go. I've got to get some sleep. Don't you understand? It's Christmas, Joseph."

He left.

How had we come to this? I wondered, what was happening to our lives, to us? What was going on? I couldn't sleep. I kept thinking about Joseph's unhappiness in the past year, his discontent with his work, himself and the future. I remembered finding him one early summer morning at his desk in his wood-paneled study, staring vacantly out the window.

"Honey, what's the matter?" I asked gently.

"I think I'm going crazy," he answered. "Do you realize I'm forty years old, my life is half over, and I don't even know what I want any more?" I sat down on our old worn, ox-blood leather chair and waited for him to continue.

"Do you remember when Jerry went through this middle-age bullshit and no one knew what the hell he was talking about? Well, I think I understand now where he was coming from."

"Is it something I've done?" I asked.

"No, it's not you. I love you. It has to do with me."

Even so, I was scared his confusion might have something to do with me. Yet I couldn't accept that. We'd always been happy together. Joseph was asking me to understand, to try to help him. But I did nothing. I ignored his plea. I didn't want my beautiful happy life disrupted, especially by something I didn't understand. And why now? We'd already been to hell and back. And, I selfishly thought, why now when my career was just taking off?

I finally fell asleep that early Christmas morning. When I a woke, I instinctively turned toward my husband. He wasn't there. And then it all came back. "Oh, my God," I recalled miserably, " I sent him away."

I jumped out of bed and hobbled down the stairs, hoping he'd returned home and fallen asleep on the couch. I searched the house. No Joseph. I made coffee. The day had only just begun, and I was already drained. I felt as if I'd been hit by a truck and my husband was behind the wheel. As I waited for the coffee to brew, I kept looking out the kitchen window for Joseph's blue truck to appear. No pick-up. Only a dull, overcast December morning.

The house was still. I was grateful the children and my mother, who was staying with us for the holidays, were unaware of the situation. While they slept, I crutched back upstairs to bathe. Before I dressed I had to strap around my hips the bucket-like brace that attaches my artificial leg to my body. After adjusting my leg, I went to the closet to choose what to wear. Since my surgery, I'd become creative in hiding the sixteen pounds of armor that concealed my loss of limb. It was a tricky and frustrating maneuver, but it was necessary if I wanted to appear slim and fashionable. That holiday morning, I selected a pair of soft, wool gray slacks and a bright red cashmere sweater. I wanted to look festive and happy. After dressing, I sat down and carefully applied my make-up. The anxiety of the long night had to be disguised.

By late morning, the girls were up and excited about their cousins coming over to exchange gifts. Mom and I began preparing pies for the evening meal. There was no mention of Joseph. Everyone just assumed he'd gotten up early and was out working in the fields. As the morning turned into afternoon, I became increasingly worried about Joseph's safety.

Neighbors started dropping by, bearing the traditional homemade Christmas gift of Portuguese sweet bread. As we sipped coffee, I suddenly panicked. Everything in our home appeared normal and cheerful. The rich fragrance of Christmas dinner permeated the house. The fireplace crackled. Children's laughter filtered down from upstairs. Mom scurried about with refills of fresh coffee. It was exactly as Christmas should be—except my husband wasn't home.

I made some excuse about having to go to the store to pick up something for dinner. I had to find my husband. Nothing else mattered. "He's probably sleeping it off in his pick-up or in a motel," I thought as I sped off. "Poor guy. How could I have sent him away?"

I didn't see his truck in the fields. I drove into town to check the few motels that lined Tracy's main street. He wasn't there. I kept envisioning scenes of Joseph involved in some horrible accident. My lack of sleep only added to my terror. I decided there was only one other place he could be—Cindy's, his favorite coffee shop. He wasn't there.

As I drove out of Cindy's parking lot, I remembered I'd forgotten about the motel behind the coffee shop. I glanced in that direction and there, parked in front of the motel, sat Joseph's truck. I walked into the registration office and asked which room Mr. Joe Madruga was in. "I'm his wife!" I said a little too loudly.

"Room 28," the clerk said, disinterestedly. "Go up the stairs and to the left."

If I could have run to my husband I would have. I'd have hurtled up those stairs, grabbed him, held him in my arms and told him that everything was all right. Instead, I had to concentrate on getting up the steep stairs. I gripped the railing with one hand and bore down on my cane with the other. I had to take one step at a time, watching my feet so I wouldn't stumble. My slow ascent left me breathing hard. It didn't matter. My only concern was my need to get my husband home for Christmas.

I knocked on the door of Room 28. No answer. I knocked again. Still no response. I knocked harder.

"Who is it?" a gruff, muffled voice answered from inside.

"Joseph, it's me, dear. Come on, wake up. It's all right. I'm not mad anymore. The children are waiting for us. Let's go home. It's Christmas."

The reply was a deafening silence from the other side of the door. A knot of fear tightened in my stomach. For a split second, the most outrageous thought crossed my mind: maybe he's not alone. That's impossible. Nevertheless, I screeched, "Open the door!"

Nothing. I started to beat the door with the heavy, silver handle of my cane. The door opened slightly. A red, puffy face, hardly distinguishable as my handsome, suntanned husband, peered out through the crack.

"Where is she?" I demanded with a sense of false bravado. "Where is she?" In my heart I knew there could be no woman in this dark, cramped, foul-smelling motel room.

"What the hell are you talking about?" Joseph yelled. "Are you out of your mind?"

"Thank God," I said to myself. But my theatrics had taken on a momentum of their own, driving me past Joseph to the bathroom door.

"Where is she?" I screamed, as I struck open the door with a powerful blow of my cane.

She looked vaguely familiar. The harsh bathroom light illuminated a bad bleach job and a coarse, white face smeared with mascara. Eyes bulging, mouth agape she stared back at me.

"I think I'm going to throw up," was all I could say.

I reeled out of the room and down the stairs. I had to get out of there; I had to get home. Before I reached my car, I saw Joseph's truck. Overwhelmed with frustration and pain, I approached it and attacked it with my cane. Motel guests, attracted by the commotion, opened their windows and doors to see what was going on. After wreaking havoc on Joseph's truck, I turned to an unkempt red Toyota car that was parked next to it. I figured it was hers.

"Oh no," a man cried out "That's my car!" I paid no attention. All eyes on the second balcony watched in horror, as I battered the little car with indiscriminate vengeance. After one last Herculean blow, my cane broke leaving me only the fancy handle for support.

The balcony audience gasped.

I looked up at Room 28 one last time. The spectators pulled back. Their eyes, however, followed mine to the window with the shades drawn. I could do nothing but scream, "How could you do this! My God, Joseph, how could you do this?" Then, with as much dignity as I could summon, I limped to my car, handling the cane as if it were still in one piece. The captivated audience continued to watch my every move in frightful anticipation that I might lose my balance and fall, a dramatic, final curtain to the destructive scene they had just witnessed.

Dazed, I drove home. But I couldn't get rid of my hysterical double back at the motel. It's difficult for a betrayed woman to recognize herself. Pain, embarrassment, knowing that things will never be the same again are too much to bear. You feel as if you may never love or trust again. You cry out at the injustice. You go haywire.

My mother was on the front porch laughing with the children. She noticed me getting out of the car and trying to walk with only half a stick.

"What happened to your cane? What's the matter, Lenor? You look like you've seen a ghost."

"You have to leave, Mom," I said quietly. "Everyone has to go. I'm sorry, I'm so sorry, but everyone has to go. Now!"

I tried to explain to Mom that she had to take the food and presents to my sister's house, two hours away in Marin County. The family would have to celebrate Christmas at Diane's, not here.

"What's happened, darling?" Mom asked, alarmed.

"The worst thing, the worst thing that could ever happen. I just caught Joseph with another woman. I don't believe it. Please don't tell anyone. You must go, now, Mom!"

I called Joseph's mother who lived close by to come and get the children. I told her I was ill. As my mother hurriedly packed, I sat at Joseph's desk, not moving, not speaking, not feeling, just stunned.

It was paramount in my mind that I be left alone. I had to wait for my husband. Within minutes the house was empty of food, children and relatives. I was alone. I changed into a robe, took a valium, poured a glass of wine and waited. I was numb, immobile. Time stood still. The Christmas lights on the tree and the fire in the fireplace were the only remaining evidence of a holiday celebration.

I waited and I waited and I waited.

I heard the roar of Joseph's pick-up tearing down the driveway three hours later. He charged through the back door with quick, determined steps. I looked up expressionless as he entered the room.

"I'm going to tell you three things," he said, "and you'd better listen carefully. I love you, I respect you, and you're the best thing that's ever happened to me. Now, if you leave me over this…"

"Who is she?" I asked, wanting to know, yet not wanting to know.

Shaking his head, he said, "It's not important. I mean…I don't know what I mean, I…" His voice trailed off.

I was praying, hoping it wasn't important, that she was only a one-night stand, not someone, please dear God, that he was having an affair with. The very thought was too much to comprehend. An affair meant phone calls, sneaking around, lying. It meant sharing another woman's bed.

Losing my composure, I bombarded him with a rash of questions. "Where did you meet her? Were you with her last night? How could you possibly be attracted to her? Please, Joseph, explain this whole ugly thing to me." His head, cradled in the protection of his rough hands, shook back and forth.

"Do you love her?"

"I don't know…I mean no, I don't love her. I love you."

"What? You don't know? You don't know if you love her or not? Is that what you're saying?" Joseph's faltering uncertainty sent my heart racing. Terrified he would say something I didn't want to hear, I gave up my interrogation. Feigning normalcy, I calmly asked if we should carry on with Christmas dinner. "Yes, if you still want to," he responded, a little confused.

I couldn't believe my sudden equanimity, my resolve to get the family back together, to cook dinner, to forget, never to mention this hideous incident again. "I have to go now, to do the chores," Joseph said, and he wearily stood up.

I called Joseph's mother and asked her to return the children, explaining that I was feeling better. As I waited for the girls to return, I drilled myself. "Just pray, Lenor, pray like you've never prayed before. Pray for things to mend, to heal. After all, it's Christmas and everything must be beautiful, bright and dependable."

Christmas would never be the same for any of us again.

When the girls arrived, they wanted to know why everyone had left and where their daddy was. I lied and made the necessary excuses, a protective habit I would use throughout the next brutal year.

After Joseph left, I dragged myself into the shower. The hot water gave me momentary relief from all the tension and stress my body had suffered. Then, without warning, I collapsed. Inert, unmoving, I sat in a heap on the shower floor. For the first time in my thirty-nine years I felt like a nothing. I screamed, I shouted, I pounded my fists. "No, no, no!" I cried out. "Please, God, no…!" I yanked and pulled at my hair, clawed my face and neck, and banged my head against the shower stall.

The water turned cold. Salty tears spilled down my cheeks. I was sore, tender, raw. I slowly got out of the shower. As I dried myself, I caught my reflection in the mirror. In the misty glass my face, so distorted by grief, was unrecognizable. Frantically, I splashed my cheeks with cold water, slapping them and my forehead. "Come on, come on," I said to the stranger's swollen, misshapen face. "Get your act together!"

We ate Christmas dinner in silence. Our children, sensing something was terribly wrong, barely ate. Yet, somehow, we got through the evening.

The months wore on.

The tension between Joseph and me sharpened. I was unsure of him, of our relationship and of his association with the other woman. I never found out who she was, and I never asked. Yet I felt her presence. I knew she lived somewhere in our town. Cloaked with an air of detachment, I embarked on a private vigil to find out who she was. At the grocery store, restaurants, shops—everywhere, I searched for her. I knew she was waiting, hoping for the breakdown of my marriage. She would be resolute. Joseph was worth waiting for.

Desperately trying to ignore Joseph's reasons for straying in the first place, I showered him with sex, hearty dinners, constant affection, anything to salvage my marriage. I went into therapy. I asked Joseph to join me, but he said he didn't need some therapist telling him how to run his life. Nothing was working. I was losing him. Our family was no longer the same, either. Christianna grew silent and Daniella no longer woke with a smile. I think both girls were afraid they had done something, that they perhaps were at fault for the changes in our home.

Joseph continued to work the farm. He went to his rodeo and irrigation meetings once a week and afterward hit the local bars with his buddies. When he came home late, sometimes I would be kind and smile. Other times I would hound him. Sometimes I'd cry. Sometimes I'd smell his clothes for the other woman's perfume. Sometimes I'd check his body for lipstick. Sometimes I would be overcome with desire. Sometimes I thought I was going mad.

The final confrontation came late one night after we had entertained friends for dinner. In the past, our dinner parties, set in our dark-paneled dining room and illuminated by candlelight, were always delightful and entertaining, but that night, feeling tired, edgy and insecure and having lost all trust in my husband, I began to attack him with insidious accusations. This was uncharacteristic of me, and our friends knew it. Embarrassed by my cruel and unusual behavior, they politely excused themselves. After they left, Joseph drove off, too.

Around noon the next day he pulled up in his truck. He walked in and quietly sat down. "I'm very unhappy, Lenor," were his first words.

Terrified, I said nothing.

"I don't know what's happening to me. I only know I have to get away. I need some time."

"You were with her last night, weren't you?"

"It doesn't matter. I've got to get away, think things over. We don't want to hurt you."

"*We* don't want to hurt you?" I was stunned by Joseph's words. I couldn't believe what I was hearing. We had always meant Joseph and me. Not some strange woman who had stealthily intruded into our lives.

"I'm sorry, Lenor." Joseph said, "I'm so sorry."

Joseph was sincere—too sincere. I knew he was confused and desperate. I also knew it was within my power to free him. "Go, Joseph; I want you to go," I said in a moment of compassion. " I love you too much to see you so miserable." I felt like I was acting out a part in a play, someone else's part, not mine.

Gratitude began to erase the heavy lines that had creased Joseph's handsome face over the past year. As he got up he said, "I'll go pack."

When he had gathered his things and came down the stairs, I got up and rushed to meet my husband. I kissed him. I held him. I said good-bye one last time. Then, I stood at the kitchen window and watched him disappear in a cloud of dust down our country lane. His tires spun on the fine gravel as he drove away from our farmhouse and out of my life. He had chosen the other woman.

The end of a relationship comes as unexpectedly as death. We are never prepared, never willing to accept, never comprehending and forever asking why.

It may be hard to imagine, but losing my husband was worse than losing my leg.

After Joseph left, I isolated myself in our old farmhouse. I saw no one except the children. My only other companions were the pillows on the couch, milligrams of valium and snifters of brandy. Gradually, I began to understand that I could no longer linger in our small town. I couldn't bear the muffled whispers, the shame. One day I was admired for my handsome, loving husband, my beautiful children, my lovely old home, my success as a writer, and the next day I was pitied because I couldn't keep it all. I couldn't stand the gossip: "If Lenor hadn't been on the road so much promoting her new book…" Or even more disturbing, "Do you think it had anything to do with her amputation?"

Also, how could the girls go back to school with the whole town talking about their dad and the "other woman?" Worse, they would have to suffer the embarrassment of sitting next to "the other woman's" sons in the classroom. I couldn't subject them to this insult. I had to get us out of town. But it was hard to act on my decision to leave Tracy.

One chilly morning in early November of 1982, after the girls had left the house to catch their school bus, I collapsed on the sofa, planning to ignore my decision yet another day. Unexpectedly, the front door opened. Silhouetted in the door frame were my two girls.

"Mommy, are you going to get up and put your leg on today?" Daniella asked.

That was the moment that gave me the courage to do what I had to do. I told Christianna and Daniella we would be driving to Marina del Rey that afternoon and asked them to pack a few clothes. Purposefully, I left most of my things behind, hoping that the frozen image of them in our house would move my husband to call us back home.

So on that dismal day my children and I, cramped in my sports car, raced south on a desperate flight to an unknown future, fleeing the disgrace and the ugly reality of my husband's betrayal. "I'll scare him, shake him up!" I thought, tears streaming down my face as I drove hard—oblivious to the scenery or the road, or the miles I packed behind me. Leaving with the girls would surely bring Joseph to his senses, I thought. Surely.

Chapter 2
Lotus Land

After eight hours on the road, the seaside community of Marina Del Rey loomed before us like an oasis. I felt relief and a glint of hope as the last rays of sunlight faded over the horizon. The girls were tired and cranky as they tumbled out of the small car. "Where are we, Mom?" Christianna asked, dazed. "Why are we here?"

"Hold on girls," I said. I needed to pull myself together and re-adjust my leg. After so many hours on the road, my brace had cut deep into my waist making it painful to re-buckle and even more difficult to walk. "All right, I'm ready. Come along," I said, as I slowly guided them alongside me to the front desk of the Marina Beach Club.

I was glad to see Sam, the president of the Club, whom I had called before leaving Tracy to ask if he had an apartment available. I'd become friends with him and his wife, Mary, when I'd stayed at the Club during previous publicity tours.

"Of course, I'll rent you a furnished apartment," Sam said with no hesitation or questions. I was grateful. The Club would be our refuge for now.

The girls and I went to bed that night cuddled together on a king-size bed in the master bedroom of an apartment overlooking a yacht harbor—a far cry from our old farmhouse and acres of row crops. We were all feeling estranged and adrift, as we settled in for the night, for the next day, forever…?

We woke to a sparkling winter morning. The sun streamed though the windows of our third floor apartment, almost eclipsing my dark, somber memories of Tracy. From the deck I could see sleek yachts bobbing in private moorings, bike paths, whitewashed condos, and handsome, sun-tanned people roller-skating below. This used to be an exciting atmosphere for me. But not now. Not when I was on a forced exodus from my home, family and friends.

I wondered how we would fit into this world teeming with singles bars, private clubs and exotic cars after our life on the farm. Did we belong in this theater of promoters and self-promoters, actors and would-be actors, writers and agents? "Have I done the right thing?" I asked myself. "Have I done the right thing to come here?" From the kitchen, Daniella shouted excitedly, "Mom, Dad's on the phone!"

He was angry. "Why didn't you tell me you were leaving Tracy?"

"I'm sorry, I should have," I said, praying that my strategy of flight had worked.

"I dropped by the house to see the girls, and no one was there. I got worried. Why didn't you call?" He didn't wait for me to answer. Instead, he asked to speak to Christianna.

That was it? Abrupt, curt, no mention of me and the girls coming home? Nothing? At that moment, the fear that Joseph and I would never get together again struck with a terrible blow.

While Christianna continued to talk with her father, I went into my bedroom and collapsed on the bed. I'd never cried in front of my kids before. Not after my surgery, not during the endless months of trying to endure the hateful phantom limb pain, not even over the past year when I found out I wasn't the only woman in my husband's life. The only time my girls ever saw me cry was when we were all watching a favorite love story together, like The Way We Were with Barbara Streisand, and I'd bawl right along with the girls.

"Mom, Mom," what's the matter?" Daniella shouted, as she came running to me.

"I've got to go, Dad," I could hear Christianna saying on the phone. "Mom's crying."

The girls were frightened and confused. "Mom, why are you crying?" Daniella asked, choked -up. "Is it Daddy? What did he do?"

The day before, I hadn't had the heart to tell the girls the real reason for our hasty departure from Tracy. I didn't want them to hate their father for no longer wanting me. And besides, I'd hoped Joseph would be shocked that we had left home and beg us to come back, relieving me from having to explain things to the girls. Now, however, I had to tell them the truth. I told the girls to sit down on the bed with me. I took a deep breath and groped for the right words.

"I already knew, Mom," Christianna said, surprising me. "Don't you remember when I kept asking why Dad wasn't coming home for dinner any more? And I said maybe he was having an affair, and you laughed and said I was being silly." Daniella said she'd had her suspicions from talk at school. But she hadn't believed it, hadn't wanted to believe it. Now with everything finally out in the open, I hoped the girls would understand why I had no alternative but to leave Tracy. Daniella tried to be support-ive, saying she understood. Christianna couldn't believe that her mom and dad wouldn't be together any more. Our separation left a permanent, open wound in her heart.

Our first day I spent most of my time alone in my room crying. Every time I thought I should go out, I'd think of my red, swollen eyes, and I'd sink back onto the bed and weep again. The girls unpacked and tried to be as unobtrusive as possible.

In the past, whenever hurt and despair would surface, my salvation was always to go swimming which eased my emotional pain exactly as it relieved my phantom limb pain. Maybe the pool here at the Club would offer this same solace.

The next day, knowing I would have to adapt somehow to this changed life, I asked the girls if they wanted to go swimming with me. "Sure,

Mom, let's go," they said, happy to see I wasn't crying alone in my room and acting normal again.

I went into my bedroom, took off my leg and put on my swimsuit. I looked at myself in the mirror. I'd lost weight over the past year, so if my missing leg could be ignored, I didn't look too bad in my suit. However, I've never gotten used to seeing my image in the mirror without my leg. I never gaze for long.

I put on a full-length cover-up, and with my girls at my side, I crutched to the Club's pool. But when I got there, I was self-conscious—something I thought I'd gotten over- about revealing my amputation to the bronze sunbathers.

"Come on, Mom," Daniella urged, "nobody's going to notice."

"Not notice?" I laughed.

"Mom," Christianna whispered, "don't be embarrassed. Look there's a guy who's really fat. And see that lady over there? She's skinny and flat-chested." Daniella discreetly pointed out faces etched with dark lines and bodies weathered from too much sun. "See, Mom? You're only missing a leg."

"Well, I guess you girls are right; nobody's perfect. And what's left of me is in good working order."

I dropped my cover-up off and dove into the Olympic-size pool. As always, in the water I felt graceful, sleek, fast—normal, as if I had two flawless legs kicking in unison. I swam hard. I swam for my kids, my sanity, my life. The bright light at the end of the pool was my focus, and with each lap my strength and hope for a future for me and my girls magically grew.

Afterward, when I was getting out of the pool, a pretty blond woman introduced herself to me as Patty and complimented me on my vigorous swim. She didn't seem shocked by what she saw—on the contrary, she said she'd been enlightened. "I have a sister who lost her breast to cancer last year," Patty said, "and she refuses to wear a bathing suit. Wait until I tell her about you," she said, smiling.

And then a young, well-built fellow came up to me and said his name was Jim, and that he was the athletic director at the Club. "Hey, you know what?" he said, talking fast and excited, " I have a friend who lost his leg in a boating accident—not quite as high up as yours," he said, using his hand to illustrate. "Hey, but, you know what? He gave up sports because he didn't want to expose his stump. I sure wish he could see you swimming."

Because I appeared not to be self-conscious, I made Patty and Jim feel comfortable enough to ask how I had lost my leg and to share their personal stories. These kind people reinforced my resolve to never feel ashamed or embarrassed by my appearance, not only for my own sake, but for others'.

A week after arriving in Marina del Rey, I enrolled the girls in school. Christianna continued the ninth grade at Marina del Rey Junior High and Daniella her seventh-grade year at the Marina Elementary school. It wasn't easy for them. Their hair, clothes, even their way of speaking were different from the rest of their classmates'. In Tracy they had attended a private Catholic school with kids they had grown up with. They were accustomed to uniforms, afternoon prayers and parents picking them up after school.

One day after Daniella had been in school only two weeks, she walked out of our bathroom with all her long hair chopped off, leaving only stiff little spikes poking out. She had not only cut it, she had also died it purple.

"What have you done?" I screeched,

"I'm sorry, Mom," she said, determined. "But I don't like being teased at school for the way I dress and my Alice in Wonderland hair."

There was nothing I could say. She had been through enough trauma over the past few weeks, and I wasn't going to let this show of independence be an issue. I tapped the top of her rigid, cut up hair, and said it was okay. That I even kind of liked it.

Christianna, my popular daughter of only a year ago, had more difficulty adjusting. She became increasingly withdrawn. I peeked in her bedroom one afternoon after she got home from school and saw her lying on her bed, with a glazed expression, staring at the TV. I knew from Daniella that some of the kids at school had been making fun of her, not understanding her silence and quiet ways.

"Isn't it a gorgeous day?" I said, gently trying to coax her out of her room.

"Uh-huh," she said, dryly.

"Want to go for a swim with me, honey?

"You go ahead, mom, I don't feel like it."

Christianna began to isolate herself the day we arrived at the Club. I'd heard that people who go through an emotional crisis sometimes shut down. Christianna, it seems, was shutting down, and I couldn't do anything to help. I couldn't reach her. I was struggling to stay afloat, but my daughter was sinking. I couldn't make things better, and I couldn't bring her father back. I wouldn't dare call him. It was too soon. I began to think that maybe she needed to go through this grieving process, and that she'd sort it out for herself. All I could do was pray it was a phase that would pass.

But God wasn't listening.

In the meantime I was struggling with my own "passing phases." Every morning I had to renew my determination not to let my grief overwhelm me, not to cling to the past that had disappeared but to look to the present for its possible joys. I was having to consciously bolster my self-confidence.

Was it only a year ago I'd been on the other side of the fence, happily married, visiting patients in hospitals, building up peoples' pride and confidence and telling them to be strong? I thought about meeting Kerry, a young woman who'd lost her leg in a shark attack off the coast of Santa Cruz, California. "Who's going to want half a woman," Kerry asked, her face stricken, "when they could have a whole one?"

I tried to explain to Kerry that she needn't feel damaged because she lost her leg. "Even if you lost an arm or breast, you're still a whole person. And you can carry on and live a full, happy life—look at me."

Uncertain, Kerry stared up at me from her hospital bed and clutched my hand. "But you, Lenor, don't have to compete anymore. Don't you see, you already have a husband who loves you."

"Yes, I know, and that does make it easier," I answered. " But you must understand: it's not what you look like or what you're missing—it's who you are and how you feel about yourself. That's what others will be attracted to…believe me," I said, with bold conviction.

Now that I was single and an amputee, I wondered if I could live up to my own encouraging words, the upbeat attitude that I'd presented to Kerry and others for so many years. And could I, indeed, compete with women who had two legs? I was soon to find out, as I plunged into the frantic socializing that was just another part of the southern California landscape.

I had all the trappings of what we used to call the "gay divorcee": sports car, luxurious apartment, a book recently published. But these superficial things only camouflaged my true feelings of loss and betrayal. It was hard to pretend I was something I was not, when I didn't know who I was any more. The only tangibles were: I was on my own and I would somehow have to reinvent myself and create a new life for me and my children.

My first trial was a pool-side party for the Club's new tenants three weeks after the girls and I had arrived. I agonized over what to wear and finally decided on a long white, strapless dress that not only hid the bulkiness of my brace, but showed off my tan. I knew that "the new tenant with the powerful limp" would attract curious stares, and I was determined that the stares would be positive.

When we arrived at the party, I was taken aback at how crowded the pool area was. What if I accidentally bumped into someone and fell down? I suddenly changed my mind. I didn't want to be there. I was turning to tell the girls that maybe we should leave, when I heard a voice say, "Hey, you know what? You girls look gorgeous!"

It was Jim, the fellow we'd met at the pool and, we were soon to discover, the son of the Club's chairman of the board. Jim took my arm and led us through the crowd, introducing us to everyone we passed, always opening with, "Hey, you know what?" "Hey, you know what?" he said, "I'd like to introduce you to our Club tennis pro, Leigh Davies," and we stopped in front of a dapper-looking gentleman in a navy blue sports coat, crisp white linen shirt and white slacks.

"My pleasure, indeed, ladies, "Leigh said, in a charming, upper-class British accent.

"Hey, you know what?" Jim said, as he nudged me. "Leigh lives on Humphrey Bogart's old thirty-six foot Chris Craft. As a matter of fact, it's moored just below your apartment."

"Really?" I said, excited.

"Who's Humphrey Bogart?" the girls wanted to know.

"Oh, he was quite famous, I can assure you girls," Leigh said, smiling while lighting a trim, dark cigarette. "But, unfortunately, he's not around anymore." He winked at me and Jim.

Leigh then introduced us to the couple standing next to him, Bill and JoAnn Stewart, also new members of the Club. Bill, a ruggedly handsome Canadian, jauntily shook our hands while his elegant, but aloof wife, said hello. During our brief conversation, I learned from Bill that only a year ago they had sold everything they owned in Canada and, with no experience, came to L.A. to try and produce a science-fiction adaptation of Wagner's opera, The Ring, that they had co-written.

"JoAnn's an opera singer," Bill said, proudly with a broad grin, "and I'm a writer who happens to dig Wagner." When JoAnn turned to me and asked what I did for a living, I hesitated. For years my answer had always been the same: "I'm married to a farmer. I'm a farm wife." Quickly, I had to think how to respond now.

"I'm an author," I said as I straightened myself up to my full height with the aid of my cane. Instantly, I saw awe and curiosity written all over her face.

"How wonderful," she said, with sudden interest. "What do you write?" Before I could answer, Bill interrupted. "Who's your publisher?

And where can we get your book? I'd like to take a look at it." I could see that my author status would be my entry into this charmed circle.

A jazz band began to play. Jim suggested we get something to eat from the beautifully decorated buffet tables. Intricate ice carvings adorned each table, and champagne and wine tumbled into crystal glasses. As I picked up a glass of champagne, half of me continued laughing and talking by the pool, but the other half of me had suddenly been catapulted back to Tracy and the afternoon barbecues that were so different from this affair at the Marina del Rey Beach Club.

In my mind I was once again at our friends' Tony and Ann's ranch for a party after a cattle round-up in the hot bleached foothills of Tracy. We had just finished the seasonal de-horning, branding, and castrating of calves and were now barbecuing the mountain oysters (to the disgust of our dusty hungry kids lined up for eats), stuffing them between hot rolls and serving them with baked beans, salad and chocolate cake. The old timers had, as always, brought their crude homemade Portuguese red wine that later warmed us up for kick-stomping under the stars. Country music was played by any cowboy with a harmonica in his pocket or a guitar tied to the back of his saddle.

For a moment, sadness engulfed me as I longed for home and its plain and simple gatherings. What was I doing here in all this fancy glitter?

"Hey, you know what?" Jim said, interrupting my thoughts. " I'm going to introduce you to the greatest man alive!" He directed us towards an extremely handsome man surrounded by a group of people engrossed in his conversation. He was tall, deeply tanned and distinguished with short, steel gray hair, blue eyes and a smile that radiated vitality. "This is Nick, my Pops," Jim said, with pure adulation. "He adopted me when I was a kid."

Only when we were introduced did I notice Nick was gripping a cane. When he extended his hand I noticed it shook. When he spoke, I noticed his speech was slow, the enunciation of each word an effort. Only when he turned away did I observe his difficulty walking.

The moment Nick and I met, we connected immediately and forever.

Nick had been diagnosed with multiple sclerosis at eighteen years of age. Told he would be in a wheelchair in six months and probably dead in four years, he ignored the prognosis. His attitude was, "I didn't intrude on MS; it intruded on me. I'm not going to accommodate MS. I'm going to continue to live my life the way I choose, and if MS doesn't want to put up with the way I live, then it can leave. I'll never concede to MS." And he never did. With unyielding determination he persevered. In the beginning, he told no one of his condition, not even his own mother.

Over the years, multiple sclerosis continued its erratic assault on Nick. "Whenever it hit," he told me later, "I would simply take it easy and wait for the flare-up to pass. I'd use 'an old surfing back injury' excuse when an explanation was needed."

After serving in the Navy, during which time doctors did not detect his MS, Nick returned to school and got a law degree. He became a corporate negotiator, flying all over the world on private planes to settle disputes. He was fluent in four languages and chummed around with jet setters, celebrities and corporate giants, as well as with the next door neighbors. His friends were as varied, as they were interesting.

After the party, Jim escorted me and the girls back to our apartment. "I hope we'll be seeing more of you and Nick," I said.

"Of course you will," Jim said, hugging me and the girls. "Hey, you know what? We live only two doors down from you. Promenade 227."

As the girls prepared for bed, I went to my room and with great relief took off my leg, slipped a comfortable robe on and went out on the deck. Having to stand for most of the afternoon on my good leg, using my artificial leg only for support, had weakened my right leg, as is often the case. When this happens, I need to get my leg off, sit down, and elevate the good leg to get the circulation going again—and try to relieve the pressure from my foot.

As I rubbed my ankle, I gazed out over the harbor and breathed in the salt air. My thoughts were of the party and of all the fashionable, well-heeled, mostly divorced new members I'd met and how they all seemed thrilled with the prospect of starting over in golden, care-free southern California. How come I couldn't be like that? But my enthusiasm got mired in the reality of my emotions. I didn't want to start over. I already had a home and friends. It didn't seem fair that I had to adapt to permanently living in a new place. Why not Joseph? It wasn't my choice to leave. He wanted out, not me. I found myself struggling with resentment as well as hurt, anger and, even worse, self-pity.

Also, I couldn't stop thinking about our old home in Tracy, sitting empty in the middle of three hundred acres of farm land. Joseph was still living in the apartment he'd rented when he left home that grim October morning. I could picture our home and the warm gracious rooms with their high ceilings, the beautiful fireplace mantel with the beveled mirror that I'd found in a yard sale and stripped and varnished, the children's room with its graceful French windows and Joseph's and my room with the grand old four- poster bed where we'd wake up to sweeping views of fields and hills. Empty now, our old home, and cheerless. But intact, as if the girls and I had just gone to town. And maybe we had. Maybe we would be back.

Joseph and I had bought the house in a neglected and decayed state a year before my operation in 1973. It had sat for a century on a corner block in the center of a nearby city before we moved it by barge twenty-eight miles down river to our farm. We completely restored it to its original design in six months and moved in, happily thinking it would be our home for life.

I looked around at the apartment I was in now. What a contrast to that beautiful old house! I had to accept and conform to the lack of roominess of this two-bedroom apartment. It may have been furnished with all the comforts of home, but it wasn't home, and these things were neither familiar nor ours. Weary, I got up to go to bed. But when I walked into my bedroom, I admitted that this was one room I did like. It faced west overlooking the harbor. At night, I was consoled by soft breezes whispering through the palm trees, the crooning and creaking of boats as they rocked in their moorings, the splashing of buoys, the tingling of sailboat riggings, and often a distant fog horn. I loved these sounds, but tonight my longing for Joseph and our old home and friends overshadowed these comforting sounds. As I crawled into bed, I realized it would be a long time before I would ever shake the persistent heartbreak of losing my husband. And in spite of my determination to overcome self-pity, my face was awash with tears.

We'd been living at the Club for only two months, when Christianna began hounding me, asking if her father could come visit us over Christmas, only a few weeks away. At first, I thought it was an outrageous idea, but the more she pestered me, the more I began to consider it. Why not give it one more shot? What did I have to lose? I knew from friends that Joseph wasn't living with the woman yet. Maybe there was a chance. "Dear god," was my thought. "Give me one last chance."

My plan was to include his mother, Annabelle, who had been like a mother to me since I was fifteen years old. I called her first. "What do you think, Mom? Do you think he'd come for Christmas? That is, of course," I added, " if you'll come, too."

Annabelle liked the idea, but she never interfered with any of her son's decisions. "You'll have to ask Joseph, dear," she said.

"But, Mom, can I say that you'll come?" I asked, knowing that the only way I could get Joseph to be with us for Christmas would be if his mother came. She would be his buffer. He would feel safe from any emotional scenes from me. And, if his mother came along, maybe his girlfriend wouldn't get too upset with the idea of him spending Christmas with his wife and children.

Joseph wasn't too happy with the idea of going to L.A. and spending Christmas at the Club. All I could get him to agree to were three days, December 23 through 25th. The girls were thrilled, and I was happy to have this opportunity to maybe get my husband back.

The day arrived. I encouraged the girls to get dressed up for their father. I, too, wanted to look my best so I wore a blue velvet top that Joseph had always liked on me, with matching pants. The girls and I waited in front of the airport terminal in the Club limo that I'd hired because my sports car was too small for all of us. The limo, I rationalized, was cheaper than a taxi, anyway. Nervously, I fiddled with my wedding ring. Then I saw Joseph, coming through the arrival gate. My heart stopped. He looked gorgeous in the boots, jeans, sweater and Western sports jacket that I knew so well. And when he brushed his lips against my cheek, I could smell the scent of the man I had loved forever.

Tears stung my eyes as I tried to remain poised and calm. "Don't show too much emotion, don't overwhelm him, don't look pathetic, don't show too much love. Don't screw up your last chance. Don't…"

The girls were all over their dad and grandmother, asking about home, their friends, their cousins. During the short drive back to the Club, Joseph's quiet demeanor didn't stop the girls from their excited chatter as they pointed out the harbor, the boats, the bicycle paths, the restaurants.

The Club bellhop helped carry the suitcases and Christmas gifts into my apartment. Joseph tipped him grandly. "Would you like a scotch and water, honey?" I asked. Suddenly I felt embarrassed. "I mean, Joseph?"

"Okay," he said with a crooked smile. He took his drink and walked out onto the deck, ablaze with bright December sunlight.

Mom and I got busy putting together Christmas dinner, while the girls entertained their dad. To please Joseph, I had prepared his favorite dishes which his mom taught me to cook long ago: Portuguese baked beans, fresh string-beans sautéed in bacon grease, onions, mushrooms and whole tomatoes. For dessert, I'd made vanilla cream pie with a graham cracker crust. We ate an early dinner outside in beautiful summer-like weather with the harbor as our backdrop.

Later, the girls took their grandma for a tour of the Club. I asked Joseph if he would like to go up to the Club bar and have a drink. "Okay," he shrugged, "I guess."

He wasn't showing much enthusiasm, but it didn't matter. I wanted to walk side by side with my husband, hold his hand, show him off to the other Club members, pretend we were a couple again. He didn't hold my hand, and he wasn't very polite when I introduced him as my husband. We only had one drink, and it seemed we didn't have much to say. Finally, I got up the nerve to mention that I'd made reservations at a quaint restaurant for the following evening for just the two of us. Joseph put down his drink, with a baffled look on his face.

"What do you mean?" he asked, his face scowling. "Go out for dinner? Why? I only have a couple of days here. I want to spend them with the girls."

His words cut deep. He had left me out like I was no longer a part of this family, no longer missed or loved. When we got back to the apartment, I canceled the reservations.

After Grandma and the girls went to bed, I coaxed Joseph out to the deck with a glass of wine. There was a full moon; twinkling lights were dancing off the boat riggings, and the night was warm. Joseph began to relax a little as we talked of close friends back home. I even got him to laugh, remembering some of the fun times we had had as a family on Sunday afternoons, riding horses and competing in gymkanna events down the road from our house at the old Banta arena. I purposely avoided any talk of how he was doing or what he was up to. I didn't want this precious short time with my husband disrupted by anything.

Feeling a closeness returning, I got up and went to him. I sat on his lap and rested my head on his shoulder. He didn't move. He was like a statue. With my hand, I touched his face and turned it towards me. I lightly kissed him on the lips. He jolted. "Are you crazy?" he said, harshly.

Maybe I was crazy. But I couldn't hold back. "Joseph, please, just kiss me. Don't you miss me at all?'

He abruptly got up. "I miss my kids. Don't you understand?" he said, faltering, tears in his eyes. "I miss them so much."

"But what about me?" I wailed, like a disappointed child. "Don't you miss me, too?"

He didn't answer. Instead, he said he was going to bed.

"Please, Joseph, come to bed with me. Just this one night, " I begged. " Oh, please, Joseph, just hold me. We don't have to do anything. I just want to be held. It's been such a long time."

"No," he said as he pulled away from me. "What are you trying to do?" Flustered, he walked to the girls' room, slamming the door behind him.

Crushed, I went into my room and threw myself onto the bed I'd so carefully made up only that morning. As I tried to stifle my sobs from Mom and the girls, the sexy black gown that I had tucked beneath the pillows fell to the floor in a tumbled heap.

The next morning, I arose early, prepared coffee and, with a sense of closure, crutched into Joseph's room with a cup of coffee. "I'm sorry for last night," I said, as I handed him the coffee. "It'll never happen again."

"Thank you," was all Joseph said.

We went ahead with our planned day to take the kids to an amusement park nearby. I watched my husband and daughters ride on the Ferris wheel together, and it filled me with despair. This is how it would be from now on: Joseph and the girls seeing each other, occasionally, doing fun things together—without me. How could this be?

The following day, before leaving for the airport, I said to Joseph that I wanted a divorce. He was quiet for a moment then nodded his head and said okay.

"You'll have the kids, I assume, on holidays and for a few weeks over summer vacation," I said, flatly. And that was it. Joseph had nothing more to add, only that he'd see a lawyer.

At the airport, Joseph's mother held me tight. "Honey," she whispered, "you did your best, but I don't think it looks too good." Over her shoulder, I noticed that Joseph was in a gleeful mood, even smiling while checking the luggage. He hugged the girls, gave me a slight, quick kiss on the check and hurriedly ushered his mom toward the departure gate. He was anxious, I assumed, to get the divorce in motion and to get back to his new love.

After the girls and I returned to the apartment, I asked them how they felt about their dad spending Christmas with us. "I loved seeing Grandma," Daniella said, "and Dad, too. But mom, I wouldn't be too hopeful if I were you." Surprising insight for an eleven year old.

"You and Dad are getting a divorce, aren't you?" Christianna said, in a chilling voice. "I thought after Dad's visit we'd all go home and be a family again." Crying, she ran to her room, locked the door and asked nothing more.

Chapter 3
The Club

Joseph's visit had robbed us of celebrating yet another Christmas—and I knew, now, there would be no more Christmases together.

Shortly after he and Grandma returned to Tracy, I talked briefly to him over the phone about the divorce. In a moment of contempt, I told him I didn't want anything—only child support and the rights to my book. I figured I'd make plenty of money from book sales, and then I'd show him that I didn't need him or his money.

Joseph agreed to everything, relieved, I presumed, that I didn't ask for my share of our home, the ranch, farm equipment or any alimony after seventeen years of marriage.

But as the days went by I had to face hard reality. I hadn't seen any royalties since I'd moved into the Club. I'd been charging everything from food to rent. I knew I couldn't afford to live in this extravagant place, and it troubled me. But I had nowhere else to go. I had no choice but to live at the Club and keep charging until my credit ran out.

My constant worry over finances (Joseph had always managed our monetary affairs) sometimes threatened the demeanor of cheerfulness I tried to present to my children and new friends. But, after meeting Nick at the Club pool-side party I felt my concerns over money, my daughters' welfare, and our new life somewhat eased whenever he was around. His strong, positive personality brought hope and encouragement to all of us.

My fondest memories during that time at the Club were evenings when Nick and the girls and I cooked Italian dinners together. These gatherings brought a semblance of family not only to my girls but also to Jim, Nick's son, who would pop in and out for a bite to eat, or just to see if we needed anything. The scene in the kitchen was nearly always the same: Nick washing lettuce, leaning against the sink for support, while I cooked spaghetti sauce, leaning against the oven for the same reason. We'd leave our canes tilted in opposite corners of the narrow kitchen and grab for counter tops whenever we had to get to the refrigerator or search various drawers to find tongs to toss the spaghetti or an opener for the wine. During the preparation of dinner, we had only one conflict: Nick's love for copious amounts of Italian seasonings.

One evening, the girls motioned for me to come into the hallway. "What is it?" I asked.

"Mom," they whispered, muffling giggles, "please don't let Nick put too much garlic in the salad." It was good to hear Christianna's laughter. Nick could sometimes lift her spirits, which had continued to spiral downwards.

With Italian opera playing in the background, we ate dinner (with too much garlic in the salad) and we talked about everything—how the girls liked school, if they missed Tracy and how they felt about living at the Club. The girls felt proud that the chairman liked to dine with us. They said they loved it when Nick came over because they could talk openly about anything. Back home, dinner with their father did not include talking. Joseph believed, as his Portuguese father before him, that family should eat, not talk, during dinner.

Nick treated the girls with respect, like they were adults. He used to say that age is not that relevant, that some children merit being treated like adults and some adults deserve to be treated like children. He said that many children have an amazing capacity for adult thinking and behavior and want to be appreciated and treated accordingly. My daughters enthusiastically agreed.

Once, when I watched Nick struggle to get up from his chair to pour us another glass of wine and could see the pain that plagued him and effort it took for him just to stand up, I wondered why he had kept his condition a secret. So I asked him.

"People like you and me, Lenor, don't like to burden family and friends with our problems," he answered. "They don't want to hear it; they have their own difficulties. Keeping it to ourselves makes us stronger and better able to cope with life as it is."

I thought about that as I carried the dishes to the sink and Nick and the girls started a game of Scrabble in the living room. I felt vaguely guilty because, unlike Nick, I had broadcast my condition to the world by writing a book about it. But, at the same time, I felt good that I had told my story, because I knew it had helped others who had found themselves in similar circumstances.

"You're not doing the dishes are you?" Nick asked as he slowly walked back into the kitchen. "I'll do them. Your leg must be killing you after this long day."

"Oh, goodness no!" I said. "I'll just do them later. Let's join the girls, and you can finish your game, and I'll finish my wine." I grasped my cane, rotated my leg around, and masking the pain that Nick had recognized, led the way with a broad smile.

"That's what I mean," Nick said, following me. "I know your brace is hurting you. I can tell by the way you're throwing your leg out. But, all you show the world is a happy face. You understand what I mean, about keeping it to ourselves?" He laughed, as he tapped my cane with his.

Christianna jumped up from the couch to make room for Nick. Then she asked how everyone finally found out that he had M.S.

"It was when my physical condition began to deteriorate," Nick answered, slowly sitting down between the girls. "When it became obvious, that's when I decided to retire," Nick said, with no remorse. "I moved to the Club for convenience, where room service, maids and security were available. The Club's gym was another reason I moved here," he went on.

"It became my center and I worked out everyday, as I do now, to keep my body from permanently locking up."

The girls and I couldn't get enough of Nick. Spellbound by his vivid tales and worldly experiences, we loved listening to stories of his early years of living it up in San Francisco or hanging out with Clint Eastwood before he was a movie star. Or of the time when he was in the Navy on a ship in Japan and kept a beautiful mistress on shore. Or of his lavish stays in Paris at the Ritz Hotel, where he would be ensconced in his suite for days, negotiating union deals.

When the girls and I praised Nick for his entertaining yarns, he'd roar, "Don't you girls know that I'm the world's most elegant bull-shitter!"

Nick was everything but that, and soon he became my inspiration, mentor and confidant and surrogate dad to the girls.

Our days at the Club soon settled into the routine of Nick coming over for dinner two or three nights a week, me getting the girls off to school the following morning, straightening up the apartment and then heading to the pool for my morning exercise. Afternoons, I'd spend endless hours on the phone trying to book myself on television and radio programs, or autograph signings—anything to continue to promote and sell the newly published American paperback edition of my book and earn desperately needed money. I was glad for all this work and even for the pressures of having to make enough money to live on because it occupied so much of my time and kept me from thinking of Joseph. The tight pain in my heart had to be shoved aside for these more pressing needs, and soon my grief began to wane.

An upcoming book tour of France, scheduled last year and only two months off, helped fill my time, too. My editor had called asking for family pictures to coincide with the spring tour. I hadn't told him that Joseph and I were separated and that I was now living in Los Angeles. Part of the French fascination with my story was that I was living the American dream. I sent dated portraits of family, home and ranch life to appease him. I was in a quandary, not knowing whether I should tell the truth. I knew success depended on the "living happily ever after" ending of my book, and, even more, I didn't want the inspirational quality of the book to be diminished by my present situation. I didn't want the French readers to assume Joseph left me because I'd gotten cancer and had my leg amputated. This assumption would nullify the dignity of my book. And besides, I didn't believe it was true. I decided not to say anything and to deal with the problem, if necessary, when I got to France.

My editor also pressed for pictures showing an energetic, healthy, and active cancer survivor. I agreed, and had pictures taken of me swimming, water-skiing, and enjoying the sunset with my daughters on Santa Monica Pier. I loved all the photos except for one, our last family Christmas portrait. Great sadness came over me when later, in Paris, I saw on the cover of a popular magazine the smiling faces of Joseph and me with our daughters standing behind us, affectionately resting their small palms on our shoulders. To me we looked like a family of ghosts.

After I had spent hours sitting at my desk, my body would become stiff and achy from the heat and weight of my brace. Worse, the phantom limb pain would severely act up. I couldn't wait for my afternoon swim. The cool water and the weightlessness of my body would mercifully relieve the pressure for a while. Those swims also offered social interaction that I liked after the isolation of working at my desk.

One day, while I was swimming laps, a handsome blond, blue-eyed teenager challenged me to a race.

"Hey, but you've got an advantage," I said.

"Why? Because I'm young, muscular and male?" he joked.

After our race (that Greg, with a show of disappointment, pretended to lose) I asked him over to the apartment to meet my daughters.

"Meet Greg Stearns, girls," I said, introducing them. "He lives here at the Club with his dad."

"Hi, Christianna, Daniella! Say, Lenor, you got anything to eat?" he asked.

We were soon to find out that Greg was blunt and up front about everything and had a big appetite—not only for food, but for life. He was a good student, loved sailing his tiny twelve foot skiff around the harbor, was an avid racquetball player, and, when we first met, he was studying to get his pilot's license.

Christianna developed a schoolgirl crush on Greg, and when he was around, as with Nick, some of her old eagerness would show. She'd jump out of bed, pull off her favorite feet pajamas (the kind she'd worn since childhood), slip into a pair of white shorts and a Club tee shirt, apply a little lipstick, and comb her long, thick blond hair. To my pleasure, she shined again like the bright eyed, spirited eighth grade cheerleader she was a year ago.

"Do you girls know how to play racquet ball?" Greg yelled out one afternoon when he saw Christianna still in her feet pajamas lying on her bed. Before they could answer, Greg teased, "I figured you didn't. Not living on a farm all your life!"

That day the girls got their first lesson in racquet ball. Afterward, they pestered Greg to take them upstairs to the Club's cafe where they felt "grown up" drinking coffee and chatting with the waitresses. After coffee, the girls talked Greg into following the footsteps of the maid who'd just cleaned one of the visiting celebrity's suites. Christianna boasted for years that she had Bo Derek's toothbrush in her possession.

Greg soon became a family member, sharing meals, helping the girls with their homework, voluntarily running errands and doing odd jobs for me like washing my car. I knew Greg was a popular seventeen-year-old who had many friends, so I was glad that he enjoyed spending time with my girls, too. I also appreciated the fact that Greg, a child of divorce himself, was sensitive to Christianna's pain. I was grateful that such a young man could sympathize with, not criticize or laugh at, Christianna's sudden lapses into melancholy. I prayed that with Greg's influence, Christianna's dark moods would blow over.

Thus, the days went by, and I began to feel I was making a new life for myself. But one evening, a month or so after experiencing the pain of yet another foiled Christmas, I was sitting out on the deck having a glass of wine when suddenly an intense wave of loneliness overwhelmed me, settling in like dense fog over the harbor. I couldn't escape the continuing thoughts of Joseph and all we had shared—the quiet evenings we spent by the fire sipping red wine, listening to Boz Skaggs, while slowly warming up to desire, to a passion that belonged only to us. I began to weep, thinking, "Joseph, you loved me once, why don't you love me now?"

Memories began to flow. The first time I saw Joseph, galloping on a pinto horse across a field, a pretty girl laughing, as she held on from behind; our first date—me in the arms of Tracy High's football star dancing at the Portuguese Celebration. Then I remembered the night Joseph asked me to marry him, as we "made out" in the front seat of his '56 Plymouth parked in the middle of his father's alfalfa field.

These recollections of youth came to an abrupt end, as the girls came bursting through the door. I immediately put on a pleasant face. I tried never to let the girls see my depression. I figured if they saw me coping, it would help them. I felt it was especially important for Christianna to see me always in a good mood, since she often came home from school despondent. It was rare that she was excited about anything these days— even going out with Greg couldn't rouse her. She usually went straight to her room and lay listless on her bed all afternoon.

We talked awhile about what they did at the gym and who they saw. I was happy to see that Christianna had, at least, gone out that afternoon and seemed to have had a good time.

The girls went off to bed, and I soon followed. But, as I struggled to get to sleep, my depression deepened. I continued to think about being alone and single.

That night I had a dream. I had two legs and I was walking alone into a crowded place. I had two dainty feet pushed into a pair of dazzling stiletto heels. A tight knit dress clung to the smooth curves of my body. I began to walk. With my feet securely planted on the floor, I moved with no fear of falling. I felt lissome and sexy, as I swayed my hips. I greeted friends, holding my head high, gliding from table to table with no need to check each step.

When I woke, I felt cheated. I wanted to go back to my dream, back to when I had both legs and felt safe and secure, even when I was alone.

Throughout the day these anxious feelings lingered. I went about my normal activities, but even my swim couldn't alleviate my misery. By evening, I knew I could no longer indulge in empty self-pity. I decided to snap out of my rue, put on my favorite black dress and venture upstairs to the Club's private Seafood Bar.

The girls were happy enough to be left alone because Greg was coming over to help them with their homework. I said good-night to them, and then walked down the promenade, around the pool, through the gym, to the elevator and up to the bar. At the entrance I paused to check the floor-plan, looking for obstacles like a misplaced chair or someone's out-stretched leg. Unlike my dream, I had to make my way carefully through the elegant room.

As I walked, I threw a wide smile right and left in a conscious effort to detract attention from my noticeable limp. This was my usual tactic, and it normally worked. To my relief, I saw Leigh Davies sitting at the bar, and I headed for him. As we began to talk, the Stewarts called out for us to join them at their table. On our way over, Patty, the woman I'd met at the pool and barely knew, greeted me with a warm smile and said how nice I looked.

"You recognized me?" I smiled. "With my leg on?"

Patty laughed and said she loved my sense of humor. "By the way, this is my good friend, Karen Winchell. She works at CBS television city in Hollywood. We'll all have to get together," Patty added.

"I'd like that," I said.

"Good, I'll call you," Patty said. "Soon."

As Leigh and I made our way over to the Stewarts, all at once I felt better. The gloom that had hovered over me all day began to fade. I started to enjoy myself and appreciate the kind smiles, nice greetings and welcoming interested eyes turned my way. The confidence I had projected as I entered the bar turned genuine, as I sat down in an overstuffed leather booth with Leigh and the Stewarts.

Other people I'd met at the "Welcome Party" and some of my new neighbors came up to our table and greeted me warmly. "Good God!" Leigh said playfully, "Lenor's creating a ruckus. What does she do? Paint her leg with honey?"

I was having a wonderful time, enjoying all the unexpected and friendly attention, when I noticed a slight, fair-haired man coming toward our table. This was Larry. I'd seen him before in the Club's coffee shop always engaged in intense conversation with small groups of businessmen. From talk around the Club, I knew he was an eligible bachelor with all the "right" southern California "come-ons": a penthouse located on the top floor of the Club towers, a glistening red XK6 Jag parked in the garage below and layers of hundred dollar bills bulging from his monogrammed 14k gold Cartier money clip.

"Hi," he said to me, in a slow, Midwest drawl, lighting a cigarette. "Would you like to dance?"

"Sure," I said, flattered. "I'd love to. There's only one thing. You'll have to be careful when we dance." I hesitated, then said, "I have a cast on my leg."

"Skiing accident?" he asked.

"Not quite," I said, smiling at Leigh and the Stewarts. I tried to ease my leg out of the booth without creating any unnecessary distraction, but my fake foot was caught under one of the table's legs. I had to forcibly move it with my hand, lift it and my leg up into almost a vertical position and swing it around from the table before placing it on the floor.

"Ballet, anyone?" I joked, and everyone laughed.

I stood up, locked my knee, took hold of Larry's extended arm. A mirrored, disco ball was flashing, whirling above the dance floor. The Latin beat of Salsa music started. By securing my knee and grabbing on to Larry whenever I felt a little wobbly, I was able to dance with him in an almost normal fashion.

"I bet you can really dance with that cast off," Larry said.

For years I'd been dancing, ever since I was fitted with a prosthesis. Joseph was a good dancer, and that helped. Most of our Tracy friends liked to dance and never flinched from dancing with me because I wore an artificial leg. They'd take me in their arms and swing me around the dance floor, like everyone else. I loved it, because, like when I swim, I felt normal, as if I were dancing on my own two feet.

Now, however, I realized I'd have to adapt to dancing with strangers and worry about them dropping me.

Larry and I danced for a while, and then I asked him if he'd like to join our table. I thought it was time to explain the "cast" situation.

When I did, he opened his mouth in surprise. "Hey, I recognize you now," he said. "I've seen you swimming in the pool from my deck."

"Yeah," I laughed. "You can't miss me!"

"No, no, it's not that," he said, almost apologetically. "It's just that my apartment's on the sixteenth floor, and the first time I saw you swimming laps I didn't notice you had only one leg. I swear, in the water and from that distance it looked like you had two legs."

Later that evening, Larry escorted me back to my apartment and at my door asked if he could see me again. "Of course," I said, delighted.

Larry, my first date since coming to the Club, and I began to see each other on a casual basis. I liked his sense of humor, his suave good looks, and the way he smoothly fit into the L.A. scene. He wasn't the rugged farmer type I was used to, and I had no fantasy of Larry and me getting involved romantically or of him replacing my husband. It just felt good to be asked out on a date, enjoy a fine dinner and good conversation and not be home alone, or even more depressing, be out looking for company.

My girls liked Larry, too. He included them on a couple of afternoon outings with his son, who lived nearby, to Dodgers or Lakers games. It was mostly "guy" stuff, but they didn't mind. The girls missed their dad, and

Larry was able to fill in, if only for the day. After one of these games, Larry invited us up to his apartment for a steak barbecue. Later, he said he had some videos he wanted to show us. One was a promotional tape of an electric sports car that he said he designed for Liberace. Another was a video of a special parachute he said he had fabricated for high-rise hotels.

"What for?" the girls asked.

"In case of a hotel fire," Larry explained. "Guests can use this parachute for quick exits out of their hotel windows."

The girls and I tried not to laugh. But, later in the video, we saw Larry jumping out of a 20th floor hotel room somewhere in Las Vegas with a parachute strapped to his back. And on his desk sat a picture of him and Liberace standing next to a car that resembled a Corvette.

A couple of weeks after we met, Larry came over one afternoon while I was on the phone with my French agent talking about my book tour, only a month away.

"You need protection!" Larry said, after I'd hung up the phone. "I'm not kidding, you need protection! Not only from your agent, but, I'll bet, from your publisher, too."

He offered to be my business manager. At first, I was flattered. Larry was a charmer and a good talker, and I might have signed the contract his attorney had prepared if I hadn't come to my senses. After all, my agent and other representatives had always been fair to me. I didn't sign the agreement and Larry's attitude toward me changed. I was hurt and disappointed. I hated being vulnerable to a man's attentions for the wrong reasons.

A year later, Larry surprised everyone when he became a Born Again Christian, giving up his outlandish, if somewhat interesting entrepreneurial projects and most of his personal possessions. The last time I saw him, he was handing out dollar bills to homeless people on Santa Monica Boulevard dressed in his Armani suit—something I guess he couldn't give up.

Four months after we had moved into the Club, Sam, the president, called and politely asked why I was overdue on my rent—an embarrassing situation, in the prosperous atmosphere of the Marina Beach Club.

"I'll be right up to see you, Sam," I said, "and I'll explain."

"Fine, Lenor, fine," Sam replied.

I was frantic. God, I couldn't be kicked out of the Club just before I was to go to Paris and, hopefully, sell books and be able to rectify my financial situation. I called Nick. It seemed ludicrous asking Nick, the Chairman of the Board of the Club, for advice, but I knew he would know what to do.

"Your only option is to stall Sam for more time," Nick instructed. "Tell him about your French tour and how it will generate money."

Terrified, I made my way down the long promenade that led to Sam's office. I passed Nick's apartment, where I could see him from the window giving me the thumbs up sign. "Dear Nick," I thought, "what would I do without you?"

When I got to the executive offices, Sam's secretary saw me and ushered me into his office. "Sam," I trembled, "I'm sorry about my delay in rent, but I've been waiting for royalties to come in on my paper-back book."

"It's been four months, already," Sam said, kindly, but a little impatiently.

"Sam, I promise I'll pay just as soon as my royalties come in, after my book promotions tour."

Thankfully, I was able to convince the big-hearted Sam that I'd make good on my rent. My pleading helped, but the deciding factors—I knew from Nick—were the faxes arriving at the Club from my French agent regarding book advances. Hallelujah!

Now, it was time to get serious about this Paris promotion tour. When I had been there in 1981 to sell my book, the publisher who picked it up had asked me if I spoke French. When I said "no," he said, "What a pity, Madame, because if you spoke French we would invite you back for a book tour.

"Oh, Monsieur," I had answered at once, "but I will!"

Now, I had to make good on my promise to learn the language. I enrolled in a crash-course in French at the local college and practiced with anyone who would listen. I hoped that with my grasp of Italian (which I'd learned in 1962 while hitchhiking through Europe) I'd be able to pick up enough French to get through a short interview.

I also made arrangements for the girls to stay with their father for the two weeks I'd be gone. I hoped that spending time with Joseph would jar Christianna out of her on-and-off mood swings.

Right up until the day I left for Paris, I was at my desk answering faxes from my agent regarding interview arrangements, accommodations and my ability to speak French. I assured her that my French was adequate, hoping my publisher wouldn't phone to verify it. I had received the hardcover editon of my book in French and read significant chapters over and over again. After memorizing key sentences, I figured I could pull off the interviews. The French re-titled my book, L'Energie de l"Espoir (The Energy of Hope). I loved it, but asked why they changed the original title, One Step At A Time.

"Because, Madame Madruga," my publisher said, "we decided it sounded too much like a dance step."

"So? I dance!"

On March 15,1983, my new friend and traveling companion, Karen Winchell, and I boarded a plane for Paris. We settled in for the long, nine-hour flight. After dinner, Karen fell asleep beside me. I loosened my brace, and with my leg half on and half off, I tried to get comfortable—no ordinary feat, considering my cramped airline seat. As I drifted in and out of sleep, memories of my last trip to Paris, only a year an a half ago while I was still living in Tracy and happily married to Joseph, flickered through my half-conscious mind. I remembered rooming with Cathy Zupan, a childhood girlfriend who was traveling with me, at L'Hotel, a curious hotel on the Left Bank where Oscar Wilde had lived and died. I also remember how excited I was when I recognized Warren Beatty as we were registering in the tiny foyer.

"You must be Warren Beatty," I said.

He turned toward me, removed his dark glasses and said, "Sometimes."

I remembered taking an ornate iron cage ascenseur up to the spacious apartment of my prospective agent; it was filled with manuscripts and books reaching to the ceiling of every room. I remembered her words over lunch: "I've already decided to represent you, Lenor, because I think Europe needs to wake up and change its gloomy attitude toward cancer."

It was just what I'd hoped for. If my story could make just one French person not give up, I had thought, then everything I had been through would have been worth it. "God took my leg," I had told the agent, "but he gave me so much more: the capacity to make a difference."

My most treasured memories of that trip to France, were of the Baroness de Roujoux, a lovely woman I had met two years before in Carmel, California, at a book signing. The Baroness had lost her son to cancer. She later wrote to me from Paris saying that my book had helped her through the grieving process of her son's death. She said my book must be published in Europe, and if I was ever in Paris, to please call. When I did, the Baroness told me she was in Macon at her chateau for the weekend, and asked if we would like to join her. "I still have so many unanswered questions about my son's death," she said, "and about cancer. Perhaps you would be gracious enough to come to my home and help me understand."

I accepted, happy to be of any help to the Baroness in her quest to "understand."

Admittedly, Cathy and I were also excited to be invited to a chateau in the south of France. As we packed, we envisioned lavish scenes at the Baroness's chateau, rubbing elbows with nobility at gala dinner parties and formal outdoor picnics. We couldn't wait.

We were late getting to the Paris train station to catch the train to Macon. Because of the great distance to get to the train, I needed a wheel-chair, but there was none in sight. Just as the conductor yelled, "all aboard," I spotted Cathy charging toward me with a dilapidated baggage cart. She piled our four huge bags onto the cart and yelled "Get on!"

Sans grace, I managed to scramble on top.

"Last call, all aboard!"

Frantically, Cathy pushed me and all our luggage as fast as she could as the train slowly began to move down the track. I couldn't stop laughing at the scene we were creating. There I was, sitting precariously on top of all our bags trying not to fall while my porter, Cathy, was huffing, puffing and cursing down the platform.

"Cathy," I yelled out, trying to be heard above the conductor's shouting, train whistles and clanking metal. "Where's our camera? I'd love to get a picture of this."

"You're sitting on it !"

We got into our compartment just as the train was pulling out. Cathy stashed our luggage, while I found our places. "We made it!" We both laughed, collapsing into the cushy seats. "Just a minute," Cathy said, wrinkling her forehead. "Are we sure this is the right train?" She turned to a man across the aisle. "Excuse me, sir, but is this train going to Macon?"

"No, Madame, this train is going to Switzerland."

"Switzerland!" We leaped out of our seats! Cathy ran off in search of the conductor. The final destination of the train was Switzerland, but it also stopped in Macon. Relieved, we celebrated with a bottle of Beaujolais.

When we arrived in Macon, I peered out the train window expecting to see the Baroness in a chauffeur driven car. Instead, a Fiat drove up, and behind the wheel was Malie, my feisty seventy-year-old Baroness. She jumped out of the car with the agility of a young woman and walked briskly toward us. "Welcome to Macon! I'm so pleased you've come."

We stuffed our luggage into the tiny car and drove off. The night was black. The winding country road revealed silhouettes of tall poplar trees. In the distance, Malie pointed to her chateau. It was so immense that even the dark night couldn't shield it from our tired eyes. We pulled up, not to the front entrance, but to a side door. We pried ourselves from the car and entered a small foyer. Malie led us up a narrow passage to the second floor. She explained that since her husband's death, she rarely used the upstairs. "There's only me now. I just use the kitchen to sleep in what was once the servants' quarters."

Cathy and I were mesmerized, as we followed Malie to our bedroom through salon after darkened salon. Musty rooms were filled with antiques. Family portraits, heirlooms, and tapestries hung from walls. Exquisite Persian carpets covered well-worn wooden floors. Malie said nothing had changed since her husband's family built and furnished the chateau in the late 1800's.

Malie opened a door to our room. "Make yourselves comfortable," she said. "I'll prepare something light for us to eat in the kitchen."

Cathy and I flopped down on a huge, ancient bed—dust flying everywhere. We started laughing uproariously at ourselves and our American middle-class expectations. After our silly schoolgirl fantasies vanished through the delicate, frayed, French lace curtains over the windows, we changed and backtracked our way down to the first floor.

In the warmth of an enormous old kitchen we dined on cold meats, warm bread, cheese and rare Macon de Village wines from Malie's cellar. Through the night we spoke of her son—his diagnosis of cancer, the shock and the terrible fear that haunted him and his loved-ones throughout his ordeal. "He was only thirty-five years old and had been married only a year when he died. He and his lovely wife were married in the family chapel here at the chateau." She cast her eyes downward. "He is also buried here."

The following morning, after our somber talk, I missed my own family more than ever. I called home and talked to the girls. When I asked to speak to their dad, they gave the phone to grandma. Annabelle, who was taking care of the girls, was evasive when I asked where Joseph was. I'd called several times before and thought it odd I could never reach him at home. But my trust in my husband, at that time, wouldn't allow for suspicion.

After breakfast, Malie suggested we tour the countryside. It was the end of summer, but not like the hot, dry California summers Cathy and I were accustomed to. Here, everything was green—so green it hurt my eyes. As we drove, on that fine summer day through endless vineyards and quaint historic villages, Malie told us stories of her family's past—the war years, when her husband fought with the underground resistance and tales of German soldiers using the chateau for their headquarters.

"When the Germans left, they took nothing of value from the estate, no paintings or silver. But they did drink most of our oldest, most valuable wines. My house, as you saw, is in disrepair. After the war, my family lost everything. Our vineyards were decimated by the bombings. Fortunately, we were able to replant some of the vines." Though Malie had experienced considerable heartbreak, she spoke without bitterness or judgment.

We lunched in the small village of Pouilly-Fuisse. As late afternoon drew near, Malie stopped at a grand old manor house on a hillside over-looking rows of lush vineyards. It was her childhood home, and to our surprise, family members still resided there. She walked us through a once splendid garden where her husband had proposed marriage and a crumbling clay court were they had played tennis on sunny afternoons. Inside, we entered a once magnificent ballroom that stretched across the length of the second floor. Tattered, yet delicate, gilt French chairs that looked too small to sit on lined the walls adorned with elaborate, but faded hand-painted scenes. "We danced here on our wedding night," Malie said wistfully. "It was a long time ago. I lost Jacques to the war. I miss him still."

It was late when we returned to the chateau and our museum-like room. Cathy and I felt sad knowing we would soon leave this enchanting place. We had stepped back into a time filled with memories of first love, afternoon salons, family traditions, and the promise that all would last forever. There had been no banquet with candelabras ablaze, no Counts or Barons parading about and not even a single servant in sight. But a more memorable week-end we had never experienced.

The next morning, Malie took us to the train station.

"I can't thank you enough for coming, Lenor. It was wonderful to speak candidly about my son to someone who understands."

As we drove off, I looked at Cathy. "She's thanking me?"

With these cherished memories of good times and gracious friends floating through my dreams and waking thoughts, I managed to have a not too unpleasant night on the airplane—and to work myself into excited anticipation by the time Karen and I arrived in Paris.

Chapter 4
City of Lights

The moment Karen and got off the plane in Paris and I was settled into a wheelchair, an army of reporters and camera crews advanced upon us, shouting questions and snapping pictures. I was caught off-guard. I wasn't prepared for this kind of media focus. My agent had warned me of a heavy schedule, but I had no idea it would begin the moment we landed. I was embarrassed, too, because I didn't want the first impression of me to be in a wheelchair. I rarely used one, only when necessary, and I thought it was important for the French to first see me walking.

After much confusion with the media, and following customs and claiming our luggage, a tall, dark slim woman approached and introduced herself as my publicist, Madame Agnes Balbert. "My publicist?" I said, amazed. "You mean I have a publicist?"

"Oui," she said. With bracing authority, she guided us to a waiting limousine. In the backseat sat a severe, but elegant woman. "This is Alexandre, your translator." Before I could express further shock, Madame Balbert read my schedule as we drove off. "We have an 11:00AM photo shoot at Notre Dame, lunch at Deux Magots on the Left Bank with journalists, and this evening a press party at your hotel and, later, dinner."

My head was spinning, but Karen was taking it all in stride, as she'd worked at CBS television for many years, and knew what getting good publicity was all about. "Relax," Karen said, as she patted my shoulder from the backseat. "I've got a feeling you're going to enjoy every minute of this."

Karen was right, and it didn't take us long to get caught up in the fervor of Paris that unforgettable spring. The city was exuberant with energy in the early '80's. Nouveau riche money was pouring in, and hotels were catering to the decadent, pretentious and affluent. Sheiks, sultans, millionaires, billionaires and rock stars rented entire floors of rooms in the many new, ultra-modern hotels that were considered gauche by the French. From their color schemes to the people they served, these new hotels represented changes in a place that was reluctant to change.

We drove up to a quaint, but impressive hotel, The Pont-Royal, tucked away on the Rue de Montalembert on the Right Bank. We were told it was favored by the literati, so Karen and I immediately scanned the lobby for famous faces.

"Can you be ready in an hour, Madam Madruga?" Agnes asked. "I'm sorry for the rush, but your publisher wants all the publicity we can get during your stay. You do understand?"

"Yes, oui, I understand; I'll hurry, tout de suite!" I said, trying out my French. Then Karen and I hurried to our room to put away our bags and prepare for the business ahead.

Our room was small and oozing with old world charm. In every corner was an astonishing array of beautiful flowers, baskets of fruits, and boxes of nuts, cheeses and European chocolates. Tilted on ice in a silver bucket stood a bottle of Taittinger champagne with a "Welcome to Paris" note from my publisher.

"Wow!" I said, my mouth wide open.

"I'm going to kick off my shoes," Karen, said.

"And I'm going to whip off my leg, " I laughed. We poured champagne and toasted as we broke open the shuttered windows and gazed at Paris rooftops and narrow, winding streets below. In the distance, we could see the old district of Montmartre in all its white, hazy splendor.

Giddy with the excitement of being in Paris and the prospect of what lay ahead, I figured I might as well enjoy this brief hurrah and do my best to make a success of the book tour and, primarily, bring a little financial security back home.

By late morning, my small entourage—Karen, chauffeur, publicist and translator -and I were at Notre Dame Cathedral for the scheduled shoot. Cameras flashed and throngs of people gathered around us. Outside the church, I posed on the Pont Neuf Bridge, the Seine River flowing below. This shot was later used in a story in a French newspaper. "Lenor Madruga a refuse' de perdre sa seduction, (Lenor Madruga has refused to lose her seductiveness)," the caption read. I was flattered that the French could perceive an amputee as seductive. In America, the press usually described me as "determined" or "well-adjusted." Seductive appealed more to my ego.

After several shots on the bridge, the photographer asked me to walk toward the church, up the stairs and into the entrance. I knew it was important to get pictures of me walking, so I did my best, traversing over cobblestones and uneven curbs. I made a conscientious effort to kick my prosthesis forward, not swing it to the side, in an effort to walk in a nor-mal fashion. Once inside the great church, filled with the atmosphere of centuries of religious faith, I lit a candle and kneeled in humble prayer. "Guide me, dear God, in helping the people of France."

Now, as in America, I knew I had to make every effort to fulfill my promessa.

As the photographer continued to snap pictures, onlookers, assuming I must be someone of importance, asked for autographs. I signed. This unexpected attention was very exciting, until I was approached by a man on crutches. His pant leg was empty, rolled up and pinned. He held a cup and begged for a coin. As I frantically searched my purse, the photogra-pher brushed him aside, too busy taking pictures of an American author to be interrupted by a legless beggar. The photographer either forgot or was unaware of the link between the man and me. I later mentioned it to him and he seemed embarrassed, admitting that indeed, he had forgotten. "You, Madam, don't appear to be missing your leg or to be handicapped. I must apologize."

I had mixed emotions then, as I do today. I struggle with my feelings when I come across others with disabilities similar to mine who seem so less fortunate. Are they without funds, family or support? Are they forced to beg? Perhaps they're in a depression so great, they can't get beyond their impossible loss? Or maybe it's true what a prosthetist once said to me: "Amputees sometimes use their disability to attract attention, something, perhaps, they've never known before."

These are hard questions and even tougher conclusions and I don't have the answers. I only know what works for me—not focusing on my disability. I revel in the fact that others, like the photographer, do not find me different. I work hard at creating that impression. I feel that the less negative or overly sympathetic attention I receive the better, for it allows me the freedom to be who I am. A quote in Time magazine is close to how I feel: "There can be dignity in denial," wrote Charles Krauthman. "Franklin D. Roosevelt never made a display of his suffering. We can all learn from that."

That afternoon we gathered with three journalists for lunch at the famous Deux Magots restaurant where Jean Paul Sarte and Simone de Beauvoir held court over the existentialist writers and artists of the '40's. An avid reader, I loved that era. I looked at my wine glass, wondering who else had drunk from it.

We sat at a round table and Agnes ordered wine. "Now, this is the way to begin an interview," I thought, smiling. I was scared the journalists were going to ask about my husband, but they didn't. The French didn't care about marital status. They were more interested in how I coped, how I felt about myself and what my plans for the future were; I was grateful.

The big surprise was their attitude toward cancer. "If I were diagnosed with cancer, I would not seek treatment," said the writer sitting to my right.

"Why?" I asked incredulously.

"Because if you get cancer, you die," she stated flatly.

"No, Madame, pardon, but that's not true. If you get cancer and are treated, you can survive. I'm living testimony to that. The fear, Madame, can be more deadly than the disease itself. People don't need to let fear kill them."

Over lunch, we continued to bounce off the question: Is cancer a death sentence?" I think I won the controversy. They couldn't ignore me sitting there amongst them, eating and sipping wine, answering their questions and, after having cancer, being very much alive.

My first day in Paris ended with a press conference and a late dinner in the small but elegant, ballroom of our hotel. When Karen and I entered, I was surprised to see that the room was filled with journalists. They were all wandering about indulging in hors d'ouvres and champagne served by maids in little black and white uniforms. Agnes motioned me to the head table. When I sat down, flanked by my translator, Madame Alexandre, the reporters replenished their glasses, and sat down directly in front of me in rows of high back chairs.

"Madame Madruga," a journalist shouted from somewhere in the back. "You chose to have your leg amputated. Why?"

"Because, Monsieur, it was amputation or death."

"But it cost you your leg," he protested.

"Yes, that's true, but my leg was insignificant compared to my life. And with the amputation I was able to conquer cancer. Do you understand?"

Before he could answer, he was interrupted by a woman. "Madame, do you still have phantom limb pain? And if so, can you describe it to us and how it feels?"

"Oui, I still have phantom pain," I responded in half French and half English. "But instead of thinking of it as the kind of pain that causes you to double over, I try to turn it around, psychologically, and think of it not as pain but as sensation—the sensation that my leg is still with me. Do you understand?"

Confusion was written all over her face. I stood up, and indicating with my hand exactly where my leg was amputated, I tried to explain that whenever my cut nerve endings spasm, I have the very real sensation that my nonexistent ankle, knee and thigh are being jolted by electrical shocks. Other times it feels like a hammer is pounding on the most vulnerable areas of my leg. And sometimes it feels as if my toes are being individually slashed by a razor blade.

"It may be hard to comprehend," I continued to explain, " but when my nerves and muscles are being attacked by these phantom demons, I try and interpret it not as a curse but as a gift from God. Because of the pain, I'm able to sense that my leg is still with me—where it's been since birth." My answer was a little long and complicated, so Alexandre pitched in and clarified what I'd said. I was impressed with her grasp of what I was trying to get across to the journalist, and we soon developed a warm and amiable rapport.

Finally, after dinner and the obligatory mercis and bonne nuits, Karen and I excused ourselves and went up to our room. We were both exhausted from the long day of activities. However, as I laid my head down on the delicate feather pillow, I felt satisfaction by what I hoped I'd accomplished to some extent—dispelling the terrible fear the French people had of cancer.

As I tried to unwind and go to sleep, the legless beggar struggling with his crutches, came back to haunt me. In an instant, I was reminded of the stark differences between us. Only that morning, I had stood on my custom-built leg against the chic backdrop of Paris, expounding on my high expectations of life to a rapt media, while a legless man stood against a bleak backdrop of poverty, loneliness and desperation. The sheer inequity gripped my chest; I could hardly breathe. I needed to talk, sort out my feelings, my guilt. I shook Karen. "Wake up. I'm sorry, but I can't sleep."

"What, Lenor?" Karen asked with a wide yawn. "Why can't you sleep— too much excitement? What?"

"No, no, the beggar. I'm really upset by what happened this morning. I just don't understand. How come I feel like I can conquer the world and it seems all he can do is beg? Why do I feel so guilty about this?"

Karen, not quite awake, had no answer for me. But I persisted.

"Karen, do you realize that there is only a thin veil that separates me and the beggar?"

"What do you mean, thin veil?" Karen asked, rubbing her eyes.

"The thin veil of choice. My God, don't we all have the freedom to choose? I made a choice; the beggar made a choice, and yet we live entirely different lives even though we both have amputations." I hesitated. "Then again, maybe he didn't have the option to choose."

"I don't know, Lenor," Karen said, waking up and indulging me. "All I know is that some people can cope and others can't. It's tragic, but that's the way it is. Life just isn't fair sometimes."

Of course I knew what Karen meant, but I also knew that everyone must face harsh obstacles in this life. No one is exempt. We lose a husband or a wife, a child, a parent, a friend, and we grow old.

Karen was drifting back to sleep.

"Please, Karen, please stay awake, bear with me, just one more thing."

I told her a story that I'd never forgotten about a tragedy that happened to a friend of the famous artist, Andrew Wyeth, while visiting with his wife and new-born baby. When they arrived at the artist's house, the baby was asleep, so the mother quietly laid the infant down in a bedroom close by. After awhile, she went to check on her baby and found her little body lifeless; she had died choking on her own vomit. The parents were hysterical. The artist grabbed the distraught father, shook him violently and said, "You must use this. Take this loss and make use of it! Do you understand? Or your baby's life and death will have been for nothing!"

"God, how I wish I could shake the beggar and make him understand that life, despite its disappointments and challenges, is about living." I looked at Karen to get her response, but she was out like a light.

The next two days and nights in Paris were filled with press, radio and television interviews. I was now feeling more confident responding in French. If I was not understood, I would throw in a little English or Italian followed by flamboyant hand gestures. I usually got my point across.

At last, Agnes said we could have a night of freedom along with the use of the limousine. That evening, Karen and I anxiously awaited the arrival of my childhood friend, JoAnna, who was joining us for a few days. JoAnna and I had grown up together in Tracy and had been inseparable throughout elementary and high school. During college, JoAnna spent a year in Spain where she met her future husband. She was now living in London, mother of five and wife to a Central American diplomat.

JoAnna arrived late and burst into our room wrapped in black mink and smelling of expensive perfume. Her blond hair was coifed and swept up in the "Gibson Girl" style that had distinguished her for years. She looked ravishing, the very essence of a diplomat's wife. I loved seeing my girlhood friends grow more beautiful with the passing years.

JoAnna and I giggled and hugged like schoolgirls and spent part of the evening catching up on each other's lives.

"When I heard Joseph left you," JoAnna said, distrubed, "I couldn't believe it. My God, you've been together since you were kids. What happened?"

"I don't know; I guess he couldn't take the changes in our lives after the book was published—the travel, all the desperate people calling, writing. It's funny, but I never felt more needed in my entire life. Joseph, I guess, never felt more forlorn. "Sometimes…" I paused, " I've never told anyone this, but sometimes I fear I'll never get over the loss of my marriage."

My friends were suddenly, sadly quiet. "I'm starving," Joanna finally cried out, breaking the silence. "We only have a few days together. Let's celebrate!"

"My publisher has reserved a table for us at The Brasserie Lipp," I responded haughtily, "celebrity hangout for the famous, not so famous and the wanna-be famous. The car arrives at ten, if that's convenient. Tomorrow, they've arranged for me to be at the showing of Chanel's

Spring Fashion Collection, and later I'll have a private tour of Coco Chanel's infamous apartment. Now if you girls play your cards right," I teased, "you can join me."

"God, Lenor, do you always get this kind of treatment?" JoAnna asked in awe.

"It's publicity, my dear. My publisher says it's important for me to be seen not only in the papers but also around town, and I most assuredly agree."

As we drove off into the Paris night, we were mesmerized by the gaiety, the lights, the movement of glamorous people; the ornate buildings that lined boulevards where figures, illuminated by soft lights, moved silently within vaulted rooms (who were they? what were they up to?); the rows of tiny cars parked in disarray along streets, sidewalks and entrances; the confusion, the rush, the merging, the annoyance, the anticipation; the lone painter, the bicyclist, and the dark gypsy with her basket of roses.

To our surprise, the owner of The Lipp greeted us at the door and led us to a coveted table, where one could see and be seen. A bottle of champagne awaited with compliments from the management. We had a ball, laughing, talking, eating and scrutinizing the promenade of elegant French men and women. When we finished dinner and asked for the bill, we were told it had been taken care of. Thanks to the gracious restaurant and hotel owners and to my publisher, I never had to pick up a tab during my stay in France, which was fortunate, as my bank account back home was not exactly the Horn of Plenty. I was hoping this tour would rectify that.

Flushed with excitement, we returned to our hotel. In the lobby we overheard the bellhop say that James Baldwin, the noted American writer, had just arrived and was staying at our hotel. I was a passionate fan, and remembering that he'd written a favorable blurb on the cover of my brother's first novel, The Rap, I got up the courage to ask the concierge for his hotel phone number.

I rang him up. "Mr. Baldwin?" I timidly inquired. "This is Lenor Madruga, Ernest Brawley's sister…" Before I could continue, he responded with a roaring laugh, "You mean Ernie's little sister?"

To our delight, we got to know Jimmy Baldwin and his transient entourage of writers, expatriates, groupies and Parisian aristocrats during our brief stay in Paris. France had become home to Jimmy who was flee-ing the racism and bigotry that prevailed in the U.S. during the '50's; and it was in Paris that he wrote his first novel, Giovanni's Room. During our stay at the Pont-Royal, we became better acquainted with Mr. Baldwin at Le Bar, the hotel's downstairs watering hole. Jimmy was of slight stature and dressed like a dandy with long, silk scarves always tied at his neck. His skin was as black and shiny as obsidian. His eyes were round, set close together and dark as pools. He was gentle and kind, but above all, one of the most fascinating men I've ever met. I asked how he and Ernie had become acquainted.

"Your brother wrote to me saying he was living in Paris and that he'd just finished his first novel and wondered if I'd review it. To my surprise, Ernie said he'd not only contacted me but every American expatriate writer he could think of. Gore Vidal kindly responded, and so did I. He even got a favorable review from Simone de Beavuoir. Your brother's gutsy, and he's one hell of a writer."

Unfortunately, Mr. Baldwin and I never had the opportunity to talk for long. Once spotted, he would immediately be surrounded by devotees. Always gracious, he would submit to questions, photographs and auto-graphs, and sometimes he would even invite fans to join him. Everyone wanted to be near to hear the affable Baldwin. His vivid conversation, self-deprecating humor and liberating philosophy captivated everyone. Few could compete with his genius or energy. After a long night, Jimmy would retire to his room and write. Everyone else would go to bed.

The next day, before going to Chanel's Spring Fashion Show, I went to a hair appointment arranged by Agnes at "Michel's," a fashionable hair salon in Paris at the time. As Michel fussed and styled my hair in an elaborate French chignon, I was served lunch on exquisite china atop crisp white linen. After my hair, make-up was applied and then I had a manicure. When my fingernails had been brightly painted, the manicurist asked if I wanted a pedicure.

"Demi-prix?" (Half-price?) I joked, looking down at my leg. The manicurist gasped, as she cupped her mouth. Then she laughed.

After a couple of hours of being pampered and talking with staff and clients (mostly about their own touching experiences with cancer) and signing books that Agnes had conveniently brought, I reluctantly took my leave. "Merci, merci et au revoir," I said, as I walked out the door. To my astonishment, the staff and clients stood up and applauded. I was overwhelmed. I could only smile and shake my head in amazement as tears filled my eyes. "Merci," I humbly mouthed back one last time as I got into the car.

I met up with the girls at the Chanel Salon on the Rue Cambon. I wore my faithful black gabardine pantsuit and my only jewelry, a single strand of long, white pearls. Karen wore the little "uniform" suit made famous by Chanel. JoAnna wore mink.

Agnes led us to our seats, front row and center stage. We didn't know what to expect. My only experience in fashion shows were the ones back home in Tracy where we housewives used to model in high school gyms on make-shift stages or at local hotels—a long way from the glamorous runways of Paris.

Suddenly, we heard a familiar voice over the speakers. It was the American R&B artist, Joe Turner, belting out the blues as rail—thin models hustled down the runway in dazzling garments with ropes of Chanel signature chains dangling from vests, jackets, purses, shoes and formal attire. As the gorgeous models glided down the runway, photographers were taking pictures of me, too. Thank God, they didn't ask me to parade down the runway and strut my stuff! Little did I know, that sixteen years later, Aimee Mullins, a double amputee, would captivate the fashion world by modeling on runways throughout America and Europe. Today, she says she wants everyone to accept her as Aimee. Not sad Aimee, not Aimee the amputee, but just Aimee. With modeling, Aimee hopes to "break down barriers as far as being a female amputee."

After the showing, we were escorted to Coco Chanel's apartment, directly above the main salon, and up the wide, sweeping art-deco staircase that Coco Chanel used to sit at the top to watch her models. The fashion show director apologized to me for not having an elevator.

"No, Monsieur, it doesn't matter, really," I said.

I'd have crawled, if necessary, to get up the stairs to see Coco Chanel's apartment. Fortunately, I was able to walk. When I reached the top, however, I had to take a few moments to compose myself, struggling to hide the fact that I was completely out of breath. And then as always "the beauty of effort" came to mind. For some, running a marathon or chalking up the miles on an exercise machine is effort, but for me, effort is the need to get from point A to point B. And when I'm successful, like climbing Ms. Chanel's formidable staircase, I never fail to appreciate how effort translates into sheer beauty for me.

Time stood still in the private rooms inhabited by Ms. Chanel for over fifty years. It was 1920. We could visualize celebrated personalities of the era, champagne in hand, waiting in the vestibule for Coco, the gypsy artist, to make her grand entrance. Dinner would be served on the black lacquered dining room table; later, guests would languish on silk pillows scattered about that contrasted brightly with the African skins covering divans and chairs. Late in the night, Coco would finally bid, "Bonne nuit," to her friends, sleep a few hours and be up at dawn working on her next fashion extravaganza.

The following day, Agnes informed me that the Nova Park Elysee Hotel had extended an invitation for us to stay at their new contemporary hotel. Their public relations woman, Elsa, a beautiful, quixotic woman and close friend of Agnes, had told her that the Nova Park wanted to cash in on some of the publicity my book was generating. My friends and I loved the Pont-Royal and were grateful for their hospitality, but who's to argue with a grand suite at the Nova Park?

That afternoon we were picked up in a Silver Cloud Rolls Royce to be taken to the hotel. We suddenly felt transported into another world, a rarefied, gilded domain. I ran my hand along the leather, as I lowered myself onto the seat, feeling the coolness as I sank into the cushion. The chauffeur closed the door softly, sealing us within. Mozart echoed against the lush, brown interior. The polished dashboard of burl-wood and brass gauges glistened. I felt like I was being escorted to our hotel in a Chariot of the Gods. Agnes said we were privileged to be riding in one of the few Rolls Royces in all of Paris. We felt like the "four hundred" all right, sipping Dom Perignon champagne, riding in a Rolls Royce with the city lights of Paris illuminating our way. How quickly, I thought, time and circumstance can be transposed. Only a week ago I was trying to scrape together enough money in California to pay for a taxi to get to the airport for my flight to Paris.

Monsieur Richard Divochelle, the manager of the Nova Park, personally guided us to the "Sarah Bernhardt Suite," one of many theme rooms. I assumed he had selected this particular suite for me because Ms. Bernhardt, the great tragedienne of the French theater in the early 1900's, was also an amputee. I asked.

"No, no, Madame, I'm terribly sorry. I hope I didn't offend you, but I had completely forgotten that Ms. Bernhardt had lost her leg."

"Au contraire, I'm pleased, flattered," I said earnestly.

Coincidentally, I had read the biography of Madame Sarah, by Cornelia Otis Skinner. A powerful passage from the last chapter, describing Ms. Bernhardt in old age, had deeply moved me: "An old woman heroically and insanely determined to ignore time, pain and physical laws, smiling and joking to forestall being pitied, shedding on the public the warmth of a radiance that never goes out, greater perhaps in this glowing twilight than in the sparkling days of her apogee." I pray, everyday that I may exhibit the spirit of this kind of courage and temperament.

The "Sarah Bernhardt Suite" had a large foyer filled with vases of flowers. A bar opened to a grand salon, complete with a mock stage bordered by huge potted palms. At center stage was a life-size painting of Madame Sarah hidden behind dark velvet tasseled curtains that opened to the "idol woman." An imposing staircase led to the second floor revealing a bath and sitting room, covered from floor to ceiling in Italian marble. A sumptuous boudoir with a canopied bed draped in silks was on the third floor. Off the bedroom was a small ante chamber that opened to the street. I asked what this room was used for.

"Well, Madame, if you have a guest and you wish him to leave discreetly, he uses this door. Comprenez vous?"

"Oui, yes, I understand. I just hope that situation develops." I winked.

"In Paris, Madame, I'm sure you will have no problem," Monsieur Divochelle responded with gentlemanly aplomb.

That evening we were invited by Elsa to join her and a friend for dinner in the hotel's dining room. "Meet Rosalie de la Torre, entrepreneur extraordinaire," Elsa exclaimed, as she and a beautiful young woman stood up when we approached their table. "Rosalie also books the talent here at the hotel's Club."

Rosalie was as exotic as her name and Mexican-American heritage implied. She was from San Jose, California, and had attended Stanford University, where she had met a medical student and fallen in love. After Stanford she followed him to Paris.

"We shared a life for many years, here in Paris, until he left me for his nurse," she said, laughing.

Rosalie seemed to know everyone and everything that was happening in Paris. "You must join me for dancing after dinner," she insisted in her lyrical French accent. "We will go to a private Club, oui?"

"Oui, yes," Karen, JoAnna and I responded enthusiastically.

It was past midnight when we entered La Cave, a private Club located in a huge nondescript building on the Left Bank. Rosalie smoothly ushered us past the guard at the door into a cavernous room with gaudy, bright murals covering expansive walls. Dark figures danced above and below us to pulsating disco music. Periodically, a searchlight scanned the place revealing guests dressed as if they had just stepped into Berlin decadence, circa 1929. Marlene Dietrich whirled underneath a flickering strobe light. Mata Hari was sitting at one of the many bars in conversation with a mysterious man, and Charlie Chaplin was waddling about swinging his cane while tipping his hat to all the pretty girls. We were spellbound by these ghostly players in this bizarre Parisian Club.

"Champagne, s'il vous plait," Rosalie ordered for all of us before she slid out of her chair and slowly, seductively, walked toward the dance floor. All eyes watched as she dramatically let her long hair fall down the length of her back. She undid the sash at her hips and began to swirl it around her body as a matador would perform with his cape. Rosalie de la Torre danced. She danced alone. She moved with the grace of a ballerina and the fury of a gypsy. We were intoxicated.

I danced, too, but with a partner, a French ultra-light pilot who had just returned from an air race in the south of France. As we danced, he barely spoke to me. I thought it was because of my restricted French, or maybe he was uncomfortable after I told him I had an artificial leg. When I asked if something was wrong, he apologized, saying he was sorry and that it was a mistake coming to this Club. "You see, I lost a friend, a member of our flying group, only last week-end," he said, shaken. "He crashed during the annual air race in Cannes. I thought maybe I should go out and try to, well, forget."

I was at a loss for words, French or English. However, as we continued to dance and struggle to communicate in mon petit Francais et son petit Anglais, we soon found ourselves laughing at each other and our efforts. He began to shed a little of his grief, and we started to enjoy ourselves.

As the evening progressed, the music pounding with wild sexy American and European songs and me in the arms of a handsome French pilot, I began to enjoy the old vibes of what it meant to be single, available, no longer grieving over lost love or husband. Uninhibited, I danced,

I laughed and I talked and talked in French (or what I presumed to be French) and got totally caught up in the allure of the evening—even forgetting I was dancing on an artificial leg.

When the music ended around 4A.M., my partner asked if he could accompany me home. "The only problem," he said, "is that I'm on a motorcycle. Is that, perhaps, a problem for you?"

Feeling risky, I said, "No problem for me."

JoAnna and Karen didn't like the idea one bit. "You've just met him tonight, they said, "you don't even know him." Conversely, Rosalie and Elsa thought it a bonne idee.

When JoAnna and Karen saw me hop behind the pilot on his motorcycle, they panicked. "It's okay, ladies, I've ridden a motorcycle before," I lied. "I'll see you back at the hotel."

We blasted off into the Paris night. I was having a grand old time, until my artificial leg slipped, precariously, out of the motorcycle's foot hold.

"Don't worry; I'll fix it," the pilot said, as he expertly brought the motorcycle to an abrupt halt. He strapped a bungie cord around my leg and attached it to the tailpipe that my leg was resting on. We roared off— my leg smoking all through the streets of Paris.

The following night I celebrated my forty-first birthday in my suite. The Nova Park hosted. Monsieur Divochelle and Elsa were the first to arrive, carrying a bouquet of flowers with three-foot stems. Where to put them was the question; my room already looked like a flower shop. Karen's solution was the bidet in the bathroom.

After everyone else arrived, I looked around and was amazed to find myself celebrating my birthday with a group of such distinguished people. My publisher, publicist and translator were in a corner of the room in quiet conversation. I thought how helpful they had been in the promotion of my book and how I valued their faith in me. My attentive agent and her daughter were talking to the Baroness Roujoux who had come all the way from her chateau in Macon. She was escorted by her daughter and grandaughters. As the evening was winding down, Jimmy Baldwin sneaked in through the "ante chamber" to avoid being noticed by his fans. (I knew that little room would come in handy!)

The hotel's photographer requested pictures. I asked the Baroness and her family to gather around me on Madame Sarah's stage. As we posed, holding hands, I was reminded that if I hadn't met the Baroness and if she hadn't pressed me to bring my book to Europe, all the success and happiness I was experiencing would not be mine. I felt gratified on this, my forty-first birthday, and I had high hopes that the coming year would only get better.

After the party, I had an overwhelming desire to call my girls. I'd never been away from home on my birthday before. I missed them, and I wanted to share the excitement of the evening. The girls sounded happy to hear my voice, but I could sense something was wrong.

"Christianna, honey, is everything all right?" She didn't answer.

"Daniella, are you still on the other line? What's going on? Is something the matter?"

My joy and happiness of my first week in Paris was shattered when I heard that Joseph had moved the other woman into our home. Brenda now occupied my bed, and her sons slept in our daughters' bedroom. Christianna and Daniella were put in the guest room. It was a clear reminder that life as we knew it was over. After my guests left, I went to bed and cried myself to sleep.

JoAnna returned the following day to her family in London. Our time together in Paris had made us realize that true friendships can endure, no matter what. From the dusty roads of our farms as children to the cobbled streets of Europe as hitchhikers during our college years, from motherhood to struggling careers, we had remained close. We understood that friends are always there to share the climbs, the falls, the bitter and the sweet. It was great to savor memories of our carefree youth, but it was also interesting to reflect on our "coming of age." For me, reaching forty-one made me realize that the past is significant and there are "edges" that can cut and scar the fresh enthusiasm of youth. But life itself is always vivid, always new. JoAnna and I both felt that turning forty was an opportunity to celebrate our past—and the promise of our future.

During my second week in Paris, my book was chosen to launch the National Cancer Crusade of France. Although this was a thrilling surprise, I was even more pleased that the French were not ignoring my book and its message. Cancer was no longer considered to be a mark of death.

Karen, Agnes and I were flown to the city of Lyon where I was to receive this honor. We had only a day and a night to spend in the city before we were to head off to Marseillles. The night of the festivities, I was whisked off to a packed convention hall where the crusade was being held and I was to speak. I had practiced reading my speech over and over again in French with my patient publicist, Agnes. I thought I had it down pat.

As I cautiously approached the podium—fearful, as always, that I might slip and fall while walking alone in front of a group of people—the crowd stood and cheered. They were applauding not only me but all cancer patients. I leaned my cane against the podium, and clutched it for support, as I joined in their thunderous salute.

After the audience of dignitaries and cancer volunteers settled down, I began my speech. Everything was going well until I came to the close. Instead of thanking the great Mayor of Lyon for inviting me to his fair city, I mistakenly thanked, in my limited French, "the Grandma of Lyon," to the laughter and applause of the good-humored crowd.

The next day, we flew to Marseilles in a driving rainstorm to meet a renowned cancer doctor who had requested, through my publisher, for me to meet with him and his patients. An important television interview was lined up, as well.

As we flew in the storm, I was feeling apprehensive, until Agnes distracted me by shoving a pile of newspaper articles onto my lap favorably describing my brief stay in Lyon along with my "faux pas" at the convention. Our laughter soon overpowered the hard rain.

That evening during a press conference at the Concorde Palm Beach Hotel in Marseilles, I was introduced to the doctor. "We're looking forward to your visit at the hospital tomorrow," he said in flawless English. "Many of my patients, who have had life- altering surgeries like yours, have read your story and are anxious to see you in person."

He mentioned a particular patient who, after being diagnosed with cancer, had refused to have his leg amputated even though he was told he would die without the surgery. "And then, Madame Madruga," the doctor said with a smile, "he saw you on television. He came to me and said that he would now agree to the amputation and the only reason he had refused in the beginning was because he feared he would never walk again. He told me he didn't need to dance or ride horses, like you; he just wanted to walk. We amputated his leg last week. You'll meet him tomorrow."

The following day we were greeted at the entrance of the hospital by the doctor and his staff. They were interested in seeing my leg, how it fit and how it worked. They said they had never seen a patient with a missing hip and leg wear a prosthesis before, much less walk. I was soon dropping my pants all over the hospital—but for a "cause noble!"

My afternoon was spent in cancer wards visiting and talking to patients and their families. I was disturbed when many patients told me they were certain they would die.

"Comprenez-vous, j'ai cancer, (you understand, I have cancer)," they would whisper.

Others feared they would never walk or have the use of an arm because of an amputation. Women were obsessed with the notion that men would be repelled by their missing breast.

I did everything in my power to encourage them to fight, not give up. "If I can survive, so can you," I implored. "And look, I can even walk." For added emphasis, I'd throw in a few dance steps and invite them to touch my leg. "Go ahead, feel it."

"C'est fantastique, c'est tres belle!" the patients would say with incredulous looks as they felt my leg's life-like texture and saw my bright red painted toenails.

Down a hall corridor I saw a young man being pushed towards me in a wheelchair. I could see he was in discomfort and pain. It was the fellow the doctor had told me about who had just had his leg amputated. We shook hands, then abandoned all pretense, throwing our arms around each other in an embrace of mutual understanding and compassion. We talked. I walked. I showed him my leg. He poked it, then jerked back, shocked by my leg's authenticity. We laughed. And he knew he, too, would one day walk again. Today, we e-mail each other regularly on the internet. Martin is married, has two children, teaches high school and he walks.

I was touched by the patients, by their desperation and their courage. I was also moved by the families, and the constant vigil they kept at the bedside of an ailing child, mother or husband. They often lived in the cramped, sometimes sour smelling rooms of their loved ones. They cooked, sewed, washed clothes, carried on with their daily routines in the confines of the hospital washrooms, kitchens and hallways. No one seemed to mind.

As we drove off, I silently prayed to God that I'd been of help to the many patients that had shared their fears with me that day.

The next morning, I got a call from the producer of the scheduled television shoot. He said he would like part of the episode to include me doing something physical.

"Great," I said with confidence. "Do you want me to ride a horse or maybe dance?"

"No, no Madame, that won't be necessary. Since it's an unusually warm and sunny day for this time of year, we thought it would be nice if you would, perhaps, agree to water-ski for the cameras."

"Water-ski? But where?" I asked surprised.

"Here, Madame, on the ocean, the Mediterranean," he said with growing excitement.

I had water-skied only on the calm waters of the Delta River in California, never on an ocean. Desperate to avoid his request, I said that I was sorry but I could only ski on my personal six-foot O'Brien ski.

"No problem, Madame. We can get you any ski you may wish from the surf shop at your hotel."

So I was obliged that bright spring morning to go out to the pier and prepare for my first ocean water-skiing adventure. We did the interview first, and then I disappeared into one of the Riviera's famous striped tents, took off my leg and donned a bathing suit and long cover-up.

I crutched back up to the pier where a crowd had gathered. I greeted everyone, then, dove into the cold, choppy ocean accompanied by the hotel's ski instructor. One boat with the camera crew was to pull me up and another boat was to pull the instructor alongside me for safety. I looked over at him for encouragement. He saluted me.

Scared to death, I forced a smile, crossed myself and shouted, "Hit it!"

The boats took off. Instantly the instructor was standing. Struggling, I finally got up, too. I could hear the people on the pier shouting, "Bravo, bravo!" I smiled and waved and then…the top of my bathing suit fell down.

"Bravo! Bravo!" came even louder shouts. The camera man zoomed in as I frantically tried to adjust my suit with one hand. Monsieur," I yelled at the instructor, "could you please help me?"

"Oui, Madame, avec plaisir," he shouted back.

He skied over to my side and deftly pulled up my top. "Merci, merci," I thanked him, relieved.

"You are very welcome," he said.

After my water-skiing feat (both triumph and fiasco), I decided to throw my cover-up on and crutch back to the hotel instead of going to the trouble of putting my leg on. Agnes helped Karen wrap my leg in a beach towel. Karen then heaved it over her shoulder—wrestling the leg to keep it in place and the foot from peeking out—and we walked along the pier and promenade, shaking hands, signing autographs and thanking everyone for their encouragement.

I love the fact that people are always cheering me on. They want me to succeed. They want it for me and for themselves. People want hope, not despair. I pray that I may continue to be an example of how wonderful life can be with an amputation or any other affliction. We may not choose our circumstance but we can choose how to deal with it.

At lunch, Agnes pointed out in the morning's paper that James Baldwin was at his chateau in St. Paul de Vince, not far from Marseilles. Excited, I called to say hello and to let him know that I was in Marseilles doing promotion. He invited us to join him for lunch the following day.

We drove to Cannes along winding, steep cliffs with the Mediterranean gleaming below. In Cannes we headed east towards St. Paul de Vince enjoying vistas of small villages spotting the countryside, and rows of vineyards climbing the mountainous terrain.

When we arrived, we could see Jimmy seated at a wooden table beneath a shaded grape arbor. A striking woman sat next to him. He greeted us warmly and asked us to join him and Ms. Angelou.

"Maya Angelou?" Karen asked, excited.

"Yes, I'm Maya Angelou. How do you do?" she replied in a rich, melodious voice. Fervent fans of Ms. Angelou's, we were all speechless.

We spent the afternoon drinking wines of the region while being entranced by Maya Angelou reading from some of Jimmy's poetry and her own writings. As the day slipped by, friends and business associates of Jimmy's came and went. Some stopped and said hello; others merely disappeared inside the ancient walls of his rambling chateau.

One man was living in a tree house a short distance from the arbor. Jimmy said he was an American expatriate who had hijacked an airplane somewhere in the Mid-east. We didn't know if he was kidding or not, but his house did seem to be a literary refuge for some and, perhaps, a political refuge for others. We didn't know and we didn't care.

Our final week-end in Paris, Elsa invited Karen and me to her friends' home in Normandy. Our hosts turned out to be a delightful couple who had gone to school with Elsa. He was the local veterinarian, and she owned a curio shop in the village. After getting acquainted on the verandah, we were shown to our rooms on the second floor.

When dinner was announced, I had to figure out a way to get down the steep, narrow staircase of slick polished wood. Karen and I were dressed in long dresses, making my descent even more of a risk.

"I've got it," I giggled to Karen. "I'll slide down on my butt."

With no concern to decorum, I hiked my dress and artificial leg up and bounced down the staircase, cheek by cheek—right into the arms of a dinner guest.

"Pardon, Monsieur," I managed to say as I tried to straighten my leg out and rearrange my dress at the same time.

"No problem, Madame. May I offer you my arm?" he asked in French.

"Oui, merci," I said.

It was during dinner that I found out the gentleman didn't speak a word of English. Ten of us sat at a large circular table with a bouquet of flowers in the center illuminated by an antique crystal chandelier. As we ate, I tried to speak to everyone, but it became increasingly difficult as the gentleman who had assisted me earlier, now seated next to me, was speaking to me in rapid, barely audible French. Politely, I looked at him now and then, smiled and feigned understanding by responding, "Oui, yes; oh oui, yes, oui," and then I'd turn my attention to the other guests.

Unbeknownst to me, during the entire dinner, he had been fondling my artificial foot, knee and thigh. It was only when I felt his hand wander further, that I jumped in my seat. He now had my full attention. Flustered, I grabbed his hand and shoved it back whispering angrily, "Non, non, Monsieur, qu'est-ce que c'est?" (No, no, what are you doing?)

"But Madame, I thought you were enjoying it," he said innocently under his breath.

This time, I had no problem understanding him or his intent. And in no uncertain words, French or English, I let him know that I had no idea his hand had been roaming freely up and down my fake leg throughout dinner.

"Jambe artificial?" he said startled. "Please forgive me, Madame," he continued in French, "but I had no idea your leg was not real." With no further comment, he simply turned his back on me and gave his attention to the lady seated to his left.

Later, as we were having coffee in the Salon, I told Elsa and Karen what had transpired underneath the dinner table.

"Never mind, dear Lenor," Elsa chuckled. "It's natural, it's French."

"C'est normale! Karen, did you hear that? Well if it's normal, then next time I'll tell him to try my other leg." I laughed, as I rapped my good leg with my cane.

During our remaining days in Paris, I enjoyed meeting with more patients in hospitals and rehabilitation centers and going to a continual round of parties and interviews. I wasn't complaining, believe me, as I knew I had only a few days left to enjoy my "celebrity" before returning to reality.

My agent surprised me, the night before my departure, at a dinner party with fabulous news: France's book club had chosen L'Energie d L'Espoir as next year's summer selection. She also announced that my book had just hit Les Best-Sellers list of France. Silently, I thanked God, and prayed this achievement was one more way of fulfilling my promessa.

How was I to know that after experiencing the gentle radiance of the city of lights, my life would come crashing back into darkness?

Chapter 5
Into the Darkness

After my two-week extravagant sojourn in France, I returned home to a happy reception at the arrival gate at L.A. International Airport of shouts and greetings from *two* boisterous daughters. I was totally caught off guard by Christianna's exuberance—something I hadn't seen since we arrived at the Club. She was laughing and talking, moving about in a fast and eager manner—somewhat like her old self, but not quite. Aside from the obvious fact that she was no longer depressed, she seemed over-zealous, over the top.

"Mom, mom, you're home! How do you like my new hair-style? How was Paris? Where's your luggage? Say hello to Daniella! We were good the whole time you were gone, honest mom," she rattled on and on. " I've got a new boyfriend, I did all my homework, we did all the chores around the apartment, Nick can't wait to see you," she blurted all in one breath.

"Calm down, honey," I said as I reached out to hold her. "We'll talk about everything when we get home, okay?" I was a little disturbed by Christianna's sudden change, but seeing her resemble her happy, upbeat, talkative old self was enough to satisfy me that all was well.

But as the ensuing days and weeks passed, Christianna's behavior grew more agitated and unpredictable. She started hanging out with an older crowd who were involved in buying and selling drugs at her school. Her grades began to fail. She started to distrust me, refusing to follow rules, staying out past her curfew and lying to me. When I'd show concern about her new friends or her comings and goings, she'd accuse me of prying. My daughter became a stranger to me and I had no idea how to handle this wild erratic personality who now dwelled in our home.

I had read somewhere that young teens who are suddenly forced from their familiar surroundings sometimes show a combination of adolescent angst and rebellion in an attempt to assert their autonomy as young adults. Was this Christianna's state? I wondered.

One afternoon, maybe a month or so after I'd returned from Paris, Christianna came home from school with cuts and bruises all over her arms and legs. "What happened to you, Christianna?" I asked alarmed.

"None of your business," she said with a belligerent look on her face. She threw down her book bag and walked right past me into her room. When Daniella got home from school, I asked if she knew what was going on with her sister.

"Yes, mom," she said. "Remember when I told you the other kids were picking her? Since the first day of school?"

"Yes, but I didn't think it was serious."

Daniella went on to tell me that it had gotten worse. Christianna's silence made her seem odd and backwards. So the kids harassed her and called her names like "hick," "mute" and "stupid."

For six months, Christianna apparently ignored the heckling until that afternoon when she finally got up the nerve to lash back verbally at her tormentors. The usually shy and backward Christianna shocked everyone within earshot when she screamed at the girls, yelling and calling them all kinds of dirty, horrible names. After school, however, her enemies got their revenge. They jumped and trounced on her. Now Christianna, along with the other girls, was suspended from school.

The day of the fight was the day Christianna's depression switched to anger, resentment and outrageous conduct. She had suppressed the pain of her father's and my separation for so long, not to mention the culture shock of being up-rooted from her world into this alien universe, that a rebel personality kicked in and she began to show and act out her rage.

Late one night, a few days after she'd gotten into trouble at school, I caught her sneaking out the bedroom window.

"Christanna!" I yelled, "where are you going? Get back here now!" She didn't pay any attention to me, but just kept running down the promenade toward the boat dock. Forgetting all else, I started to run after her. I stopped in my tracks, realizing I'd never be able to chase after my daughter, no matter what the circumstance. I felt helpless. After an unmerciful month of not being able to restrain Christianna, I gave up. With a sense of confusion and incompetence, I called Joseph. I told him of Christianna's unprecedented behavior, explaining that I was unable to control her and needed his help. He agreed. I packed Christianna's bags and shipped her back to Tracy, praying that Joseph's influence would make a difference in her attitude; that she'd stabilize and be able to come back home.

Christianna was overjoyed with my decision, because she was going back to Tracy to be with her friends and attend Tracy High School. But when she got there, nothing was the same—not her home, school or her friends. She entered what she later called, "the worst time of my life.'

The strain of living under the same roof with Brenda, Joseph's new partner, and her sons, was more then Christianna could endure in her confused, frenetic state. She took it personally that her dad had moved the other family into her childhood home. She thought he had substituted them for us. She longed for things to be as they were.

Brenda did make an effort to be nice. When Christianna didn't respond to her overtures, she tried to bribe her friendship by buying her new blue jeans, little tank tops and her first carton of *Marlboro Red* cigarettes. She thought if Christianna learned to smoke—with her— maybe they'd have a chance to bond. But, Christianna felt she didn't have anything in common with Brenda or her sons. She thought the teenage boys treated her with disdain, like she was a guest in *their* house. In her eyes, they relished sleeping in her old bedroom and that *their* mother was now the "woman of the house."

Tracy High School wasn't what Christianna had expected. She had looked forward all her life to going to the high school where her mom and dad had graduated. There, she would be free of the restraints of her Catholic grammar school and could be a high school cheerleader, go to football games and after-school dances. She couldn't wait to see all her old friends.

Surprisingly, these old friends ignored her. Maybe they rejected her because she'd been away, living in LA, and wasn't the Christianna they remembered. The girl they had grown up with lived in a grand old house with happily married parents who were popular and active in the community and were close friends with their fathers and mothers. Now, they considered Christianna to be an outsider, living in the same fine old house, but under a whole different set of circumstances. None of Christianna's friends knew who Brenda was, only that she was a local bartender who had taken the place of Christianna's mother. Kids can be as snobbish as their parents.

To be accepted, Christianna thought she would have to redefine herself. She cut her beautiful long hair into a heavy-metal spike style and began intimidating her old friends by implying that they were just a bunch of 'country bumpkins.' When her tactics didn't work, she found another crowd to fit in with—the teenagers who drank and smoked pot. She thought she could belie her former self by hanging out with the losers and be like them.

After football games, when she was supposed to be at the school dances, she'd sneak out of the gym and head for the river with her new friends to drink and party. When they figured it was about time for the dance to end, they'd all hop into someone's old car and head back into town just in time for their parents to pick them up, none the wiser.

Tracy is a small town, and, as in every small town, people talk. Ugly rumors began to circulate at school about Christianna, and, because of the kids she was hanging out with, her old friends started calling her names like slut, tramp, and druggie. When Joseph heard the names and other disturbing things being said about her, he became infuriated. He still held on to the Old World Latin values that daughters shouldn't drink or smoke and that they remain virginal and untouched until marriage. Disgraced by what he heard and frustrated by not knowing what to believe, he began confronting her yelling and screaming—something he had never done before. Every time he'd hear a rumor or she'd irritate him, he would ground her.

Christianna was hurt and confused by her father's punishment, as he had always loved and trusted her. From the time Christianna was a small child, she would tag after her father while he irrigated the fields, or ride beside him on his tractor whenever she had a chance. When she would see him saddling up his horse, she would beg to go roping with him. Christianna had always been closer to him than Daniella, who was a typical "little mommie's girl."

After her dad grounded her, she felt alone, and, worse, she felt trapped.

She never left her room, except to go to school. After school, she'd come straight home, go to her room, slam the door, open a pack of cigarettes, pick up the phone, call someone and talk. She'd talk, incessantly, about me and Daniella and about moving back to LA

She became obsessed with family pictures and pasted them all over the walls of her room. She cut out scenes of L.A. from newspapers and magazines and stuck them in between the pictures. Her room became a shrine to me, Daniella and LA. Her loneliest and saddest days were whenever she received a letter from one of us, and she would cry for hours. She couldn't understand why we wouldn't let her live with us anymore, and why we didn't go to Tracy to pick her up and take her home.

Christianna had been very adept at hiding the fact that she was so unhappy. Her dad and I rarely spoke, and when we did, our conversations were brief, Joseph saying only that Christianna was fine. Whenever Christianna and I spoke over the phone, it was always about her new friends, her short hair style, what she wore to school that day—normal teenage girl stuff—nothing about missing me and Daniella or wanting to come back home.

She never mentioned what was really going on in her life because she was ashamed by the crowd she was hanging out with. Also, she didn't want me to find out that her old friends now shunned her. She thought that I wouldn't understand, and that I'd ask for an explanation that she wasn't prepared to give. So, I left things as they were, thinking that Christianna was getting along okay and that Joseph was, apparently, doing a better job of handling her then I'd been able to.

Eight months after moving to Tracy, feeling completely miserable and unloved, Christianna packed two suitcases. In them were all her possessions, including her stuffed toys. She headed toward the freeway, walking across her dad's open fields to the 205 Highway. Her plan was to hitchhike to L.A.

She didn't make it. Her dad spotted her, lost and forlorn, standing beside the freeway. He skidded his truck to a stop and angrily told her to get in. When they got back to the house, Joseph, at his wits' end, called the police. They came, handcuffed her and put her in the back seat of the police car. Christianna felt totally forsaken, by her father and by me. If I had only known.

She was behind bars for eight hours in Juvenile Hall. The guards took her purse, stripped her of her jewelry and shoved her in a cell with a mix of all kinds of young criminals—robbers, car thieves, and rapists. When they asked Christianna what she'd done to be put away, she said she'd run away from home. They laughed. She spent four hours in the crowded cell; then she was put into isolation where she remained another four hours. Apparently, Joseph along with the authorities, thought that extreme measures were necessary in order to shake her up—to make her understand that running away was not acceptable.

After her brief detention, Joseph grounded her, indefinitely.

Once again, Christianna's world was gone. The shock and disappointment was overwhelming, and during the long and lonely hours

Christianna spent in her room, major depression set in. All she could think about were memories of her old life in Tracy and of me and Daniella—and about suicide. She had so much pain built up inside her that she thought if she tried to kill herself, maybe her dad or I would realize that she needed help.

Only a week after Juvenile Hall, Christianna went to her father's medicine cabinet, took one pill from every prescription bottle she could find, walked downstairs and told her dad what she'd done. Joseph called me immediately.

"Lenor, I don't know what to do!" he said, frantically. "Christianna has just taken a whole lot of pills, she's talking non-stop—irrational and crazy! I just got her out of Juvenile Hall. I don't know what to do with her!"

"Call Dr. Brakovec," I said. "He'll know exactly what to do. And call me back as soon as possible."

Over the phone, I could hear Christianna in the background. "Mommy, mommy, please come and get me. Help, help, help! I want to be with you and Daniella," she repeated over and over again. My heart broke listening to the cries of my daughter. And after hearing that Christianna had been in Juvenile Hall, I was horrified. My God, I had no idea things had gotten so bad. What had gone wrong? How had things gotten so out of hand—and without my knowing?

Within the hour Joseph called back to say that Dr. Brakovec, our long-time family physician who'd seen us through our children's cuts and bruises, Joseph's various farm injuries, and my illness, had told him to take Christianna immediately to the psychiatric center in Stockton. "She'll be evaluated," Dr. Brakovec said, "and then we'll take it from there."

I caught a plane to Stockton and met Joseph at the hospital. This was our first face-to-face encounter since Christmas at the Club, but we had nothing personal to say to each other. Christianna was our only concern.

Alone, I walked into Christianna's room. She was asleep and looked peaceful. But a nurse was hovering over her. I asked if Christianna was okay.

"Oh, yes, she's all right now," the nurse said. And then she told me that when Christianna was admitted into the hospital, she had everyone concerned. "She was in an agitated state—hard to control and babbling and chattering nonsensically. Her father mentioned that she hadn't slept in days, so the doctor prescribed benzodiazapnes, which are a commonly used tranquilizer for agitation." The nurse walked toward me and kindly took my arm. "She should be out for the rest of the afternoon. Maybe you should get some sleep, too. I heard you flew in from Los Angeles."

Sleep? How could I sleep not knowing what was going on with my daughter? Was she going to be helped? And if so, how? Like a zombie, I walked across the street to a small motel and rented a room. I called the nurse and asked her to call me the minute Christianna woke up.

Around 8:00PM my phone rang. I rushed over to the hospital. Christianna was up and wide awake. "Mom, mom, you came," she said in a brittle, unfamiliar voice. And then, completely ignoring me, she recklessly starting moving around the room and, once again, started talking in a muddled and incoherent way.

"Christianna, honey, please calm down, dear," I said, scared by the scene I was witnessing. I tried to approach her, touch her, hold her, tell her how much I loved her and that everything was going to be all right. But she wasn't listening and she didn't want to be near me. Why couldn't she hear me?

After a while, the nurse came in and gave her some medication. Within seconds, Christianna was asleep. I sat down beside her bed and began to gently rub her forehead (something she always liked me to do) hoping that she'd get some rest. But within minutes, even with the powerful drug she had been given, she abruptly sat up, eyes wide open, leaped out of bed, and yanked off her hospital gown and put on her street clothes, layer on top of layer of tee shirts, sweaters and coats. She rushed to the mirror, combed and tugged at her hair in a wanton, careless way. She stopped, not moving, just staring fixated by her image in the mirror. Then she tore off the sheaths of clothing, jumped back into bed, tightly squeezed her eyes shut, causing her small forehead to line and wrinkle up like a little old lady's, and went...somewhere.

Day after day, hour after hour, sometimes through the night, this frightening performance continued. Helpless, all I could do was stay near her, hum her favorite childhood lullabies, tell her how much I loved her and pray—pray that she'd go to sleep and wake up Christianna again.

I felt as if my world was coming apart, just as Christianna's had. "I lost my leg, my husband...Please, dear God," I begged, "don't let me lose my daughter. This I couldn't bear."

Joseph, overwrought and full of concern, came every day to the hospital. Sometimes we'd sit beside Christianna together, never saying much—just being there trying to comfort her in any way we could. Joseph would stay for as long as he could and then say, "I've got to get back home." And then every concern for Christianna was momentarily replaced by a sudden sense of abandonment. This wasn't the way it was supposed to be. Here we were with our daughter, and Joseph was leaving us to go home. Why weren't we going home together? Why was he leaving Christianna and me behind?

And then I was furious with myself. How could I still be thinking about Joseph in that way? After his humiliating rejection of me at Christmas, and after my fabulous trip to Paris, I thought I had overcome any desire to return to my old life. How could I fall into this emotional trap again? Was my love for Joseph this powerful? And, anyway at this moment, Christianna's condition made all these old feelings seem petty and selfish. She was the one in a real crisis, in real need of help. I had to get over my aching heart sooner or later.

After four days of exhaustive physical and mental tests, Christianna was diagnosed as clinically depressed. Doctors told us we should feel lucky with this result, as they'd been afraid she was showing early signs of schizophrenia. A clinically depressed person, they said, could be successfully treated with short-term counseling and medications. Because she was so young, doctors said she would probably grow out of it, and that if she continued to take her prescribed medications and received counseling, the depression would ease and she could, eventually, be weaned off all drugs. When we were told that her depression had probably been triggered by the shock of our divorce, I think Joseph and I both felt responsible. I know that we both were broken-hearted, though we never talked about it.

Still scared and puzzled by Christianna's behavior, Joseph and I questioned the doctor further. He explained to us, that a person under such severe stress and being so depressed, with no perceived support system, can often exhibit psychotic symptoms. "It's sometimes called a 'brief reaction psychosis,'" he went on. "It's a human response to extraordinary stress that a person can't handle or understand. The solution becomes for the human mind to withdraw from painful reality."

Only two weeks after Christianna was admitted into the hospital in a psychotic state, her behavior had been incredibly reversed by counseling and anti-depressants. She was a little fragile, but on the mend. It was a miracle.

When I told Christianna of her diagnosis, she was happy because she said that the doctors had justified her behavior. "I don't know why I was acting that way, mom," Christianna said, as we were packing her suitcase. "I didn't know who I was anymore and it really scared me." Now, you and dad won't think I'm an awful, terrible kid. I knew I wasn't. I knew I wasn't crazy, either."

I held out my arms and Christianna came to me. We held each other for a very long time.

Joseph and I agreed that Christianna should return home with me. So on a beautiful spring day, Christianna and I boarded a plane for LA, holding hands, laughing and joking together. It was a beautiful moment, and I silently thanked God for bringing my daughter back from the darkness.

Book tour in France.

With the Baroness and family.

Lenor with Karen, James Baldwin and JoAnna in Paris.

Lenor water skiing.

Television interview

Lenor, Trey, and "Big E" editing TV pilot.

Santa Cruz years, Elliot and Daniella.

Lenor and Roy on their Wedding Day.

Daniella and Elliott.

Lenor, Nick, Robbie and Al at Robbie's graduation.

Christianna and Eddie's Wedding.

Roy and Lenor.

Judy, just weeks before passing away.

Roy, Lenor and sister Diane.

Diane, Lenor and LouAnn.

Roy and Lenor in the '59 Corvette.

Lenor, Christianna, Daniella, New Years 2000.

Writer's Salon; Melinda, Amy and Lenor.

At home in Oregon.

Chapter 6
Some Good Years

At Nick's suggestion, I enrolled Christianna in the Santa Monica alternative school called, "Smash." Although she had missed a lot of school and lost grade credits, at Smash, she was able to make up for lost time by working at her own pace.

Christianna was recovering. She was feeling and acting balanced again. She continued taking her medication and went into therapy. She liked her new school and her teachers; educators who didn't pressure students and didn't mind being called by their first names. She made many new friends, stopped smoking and drinking and made no more attempts at running away or acting unruly or disobedient. Thankfully, everything was coming into place and, finally, making sense to Christianna.

But now I had to approach Sam once again for a rent extension. Embarrassed, I entered his office with a handful of newspaper clips, magazine articles and a new book club contract from France as vouchers. "Okay, Lenor, okay," Sam said, shaking his head. "I've talked to Nick, and he validates everything you say. I'll give you more time, but please keep me posted." With this tentative reprieve, the girls and I were able to carry on with comfort in the fact that we still had a roof over our heads.

And then one day, shortly after I had gone through this jarring meeting with Sam, I opened the mail and found Joseph and my final divorce papers, lacking only my signature. Joseph and I and our attorneys had only met once since I had left Tracy that icy, cold November morning. At the meeting, over a year ago in Stockton, Joseph sat across the room from me in a distant corner with his head bowed and no expression on his face. The terms of the divorce were not difficult to work out: I agreed to leave our home and farm to Joseph; I would receive no alimony but would get $500 a month child support and would keep the rights to my book. When all the arrangements had been worked out and the meeting seemed to be over, Joseph's lawyer, who had been tapping his pen through- out the discussion, suddenly stood up and, pointing his finger at me, said, "Why don't you get a JOB, Mrs. Madruga?" This derogatory comment with its accompanying belittling gesture left me humiliated and flabbergasted. And Joseph did nothing. Always before, he would have spoken in my defense. Now, after being my love and protector for over half my life, he let his lawyer's wrath and unfair question hang in the air. It was Joseph's final betrayal.

Now I had the final divorce decree in my hand. I read it, signed it, sent back the original, and stuffed a copy, along with my emotions, in the desk drawer, which I shut firmly. It was over.

Against all odds, the next two years were happy ones for all of us. I was at last feeling like I had created a new life for myself. Daniella had adjusted to her parents' divorce with little difficulty and had come to love L.A. and living at the Club, and, now with Christianna back home, taking her medication and no longer plagued by shifting moods, we were able to resume a normal family life.

My financial situation was still tenuous, though, and I knew I needed to find another source of income. Nick suggested lecturing. "You could get a fee, sell books and motivate people at the same time," he told me. "Call on some of those old speaking contacts and get some referrals."

This good advice led directly to several engagements. Some paid a nice fee, but even for those that didn't, I could usually make money by selling books. My first booking was at a sorority convention at the University of Pacific in Stockton, California. The president of the sorority said they had chosen me to speak because my book was not only motivational but also evoked a true love story. I fretted for days over *if* or *how* I was going to approach the subject of Joseph's and my divorce. Again, as in Europe, I felt like my story would lose its encouraging tone if I divulged the sad truth. So, as I stood that hot sultry afternoon in the auditorium for my forty-five-minute presentation leaning against the podium, favoring my good leg, I told the story as it happened, but not revealing what occurred after "the happily ever after" ending of my book. It was difficult. At times, I was hardly able to get the words out of my mouth, when I spoke of Joseph's love and devotion during that horrific time.

As I told about discovering the cancerous lump on my thirty-second birthday, the subsequent amputation, the pain, the morphine addiction, the recovery and, finally, the period when I was able to get back on my feet and back into the mainstream of life, I saw the impact my story had on the audience. Some people responded with horror, others with sadness, and some even cried. But as I wound up my speech, I could hear spurts of laughter and then cheers. At the close, I received the greatest reward—the face of hope.

I discovered that I loved lecturing. I liked reassuring people that no matter how difficult a situation may be they, too, can carry on. And lecturing changed me. It was wonderful to think that because of my experience, I could make a difference in people's lives. This was not only an awesome notion but a humbling one. I often wondered, if I hadn't got cancer, would I have been able to change lives for the better? A girlfriend said to me only recently, "because you accept your situation and are able to talk about it, others are helped. And that's why God took *your* leg, Lenor," she said, laughing, "instead of mine."

After my first lecture, I thought about ways in which I could reach an even broader audience and bring in more income at the same time. *Family Circle* magazine came to mind. They had already printed a 5,000 word condensation of my first book the summer of 1979, and now I decided to write and submit an article about Melanie Byers who had written to me in 1980 describing her battle against cancer. Two years later, I met Melanie in person at an American Cancer convention in Indianapolis, where I was the speaker. As I was preparing to leave, a tall, beautiful, raven-hair girl approached. She wore a long printed skirt, trying to conceal the fact she had only one leg. She introduced herself as, Melanie, saying she had sent me a letter after reading my book. At the time, she said, she was facing death, but my story had given her the will to live, despite the fact that her entire left leg had recently been amputated and she was suffering from the hostile effects of chemotherapy—and despite the fact that her prognosis for survival was nil.

"Do you remember my letter and pictures I sent to you?" she asked timidly.

I remembered her letter, but I didn't remember seeing a picture of the young woman who was standing before me. The pictures I'd received showed a hollow, pale, drained face staring blankly at a camera. Another picture revealed a one-legged girl lying flat on a bed, seemingly without strength or desire to hold up what was left of a skeletal body. The last photograph exposed a hairless, stone-like head. No, I didn't recognize Melanie, nor could I quite believe it was she before me. I thought she had died.

Melanie told me of her miraculous remission that day in Indianapolis and that my experience had given her the courage to search for an artificial leg. What Melanie found in the "Geppetto" workshops was what most amputees found back in the early '80's: ugly, heavy, plastic, toy- like limbs that sometimes didn't even resemble a leg. Melanie made every effort to wear the unattractive leg that was built for her, but after weeks of trying to walk, she finally gave up. She refused to wear the morbid appliance that looked nothing like her original leg. She hid it in the closet behind her long winter coat.

I have seen many amputees in wheel-chairs or clinging to crutches who have prosthetic limbs hidden away. I call them "closet amputees," because after unsuccessful attempts at wearing a leg, they give up, often feeling ashamed and blaming themselves for the leg not working properly.

After our meeting, Melanie came to California where my prosthetist designed and built a magnificent replica of her former leg. It was strong, comfortable and attractive, the leg Melanie had dreamed of.

Writing Melanie's story gave me great satisfaction. It confirmed once again that my encounter with great physical loss could inspire others who face sudden, dramatic, "not supposed to happen to me" changes in their lives, too. Now it would give me additional satisfaction (and a little money in my pocket), if *Family Circle* would accept the story.

A month after I sent Melanie's s story off, Daniella and Christianna came rushing through the door with the mail. "Mom," Daniella shouted, "you got a letter from *Family Circle*! Maybe they bought your story. Hurry up, mom, open it!"

Nervously, I opened the envelope. The girls could tell that the news was good. The magazine had picked up my story.

"My God," I gasped, "they paid me a buck a word!"

"Why didn't you write more words?" Christianna asked, laughing.

We celebrated that night at our favorite Mexican restaurant near the beach and had a grand old time.

The next morning, however, Daniella staggered into my room looking like death. She pointed out dark black circles under her eyes and placed my hand on her forehead so I could feel its heat. Dramatically, she groaned, doubled over, covered her mouth and ran to the bathroom where horrible sounds emanated—gagging, hacking, choking, coughing, and then flushing, flushing and more flushing of the toilet—commotion vile enough to convince me that Daniella was too sick to go to school.

But Daniella, who had always hated school, wasn't sick, only sneaky. Time after time she played this trick, feigning dark circles under her eyes by smudging them with black ink from the morning paper, affecting a high fever by putting a thermometer to a hot light bulb, and simulating vomiting by chewing up some food, holding it for as long as she could, then making a mad dash for the toilet. Duped every time, I kept my "sick" daughter home from school. She would sleep the rest of the morning and around noon come to me, a little shaky, but with assurances that she was feeling better. She would then suggest that a sauna and hot tub would be the final cure-all. I'd agree, and once out of sight, Daniella would skip off to the gym, grinning all the way.

I never worried much about these sudden illnesses because Daniella would recover much too rapidly for me to think she was seriously ill, so these quick little "sick" episodes remained small storms on otherwise smooth seas of our years at the Club.

One of the main things that made those years such happy ones for the girls and me was the great group of friends that gathered around us. What a cast of colorful characters, what a circle of protective, comforting and loving friends we found traipsing through our apartment and our lives. Indeed, many of these friends came into our lives and stayed there, even after we left Marina del Rey.

The Gordons, Al and Robbie, were such a couple. Long time friends of Nick's, they seemed to epitomize what people can be and accomplish in life. They had both recently retired from their family -owned women's fashion line after forty years of business. Then Robbie had entered UCLA and graduated—at age 75!—with a degree in sociology. Besides school, Robbie found time to volunteer at hospitals, work with young people in suicide prevention, and prepare and deliver savory meals for the needy and infirm. When we first met, in 1983, Robbie helped me and my girls by mothering us, being our friend and spreading her generosity. We were often the grateful recipients of discarded clothes, not only from Robbie's fashion line, but also from some of her friends' stores in LA's downtown garment district.

And Al, in his early eighties, didn't let retirement be an excuse to retire from life either. He played tournament tennis, taught in-line skating to the neighbor kids and played piano for the "old folks" at the local convalescent hospital. Robbie and Al are the living embodiment of their philosophy that no one should sit back in retirement but should continue to find purpose in life.

A poignant connection between the Gordons and me was through their son, Peter, who had nearly lost his leg when it was struck by his airplane propeller. When he read my book, Robbie told me, he had been motivated to carry on with his hopes and plans of becoming an airline pilot even with his severely damaged leg. A few years ago, when *One Step at a Time* had gone out of print, Robbie offered to self-publish a soft-cover edition for me because, she said, she wanted to see that my book stayed available for others who, like Peter, needed encouragement when something went terribly wrong in their lives and they could see no way out. *One Step At A Time* continues to sell today because of Robbie's efforts.

Venus, a beautiful, intelligent Asian woman was the eccentric romantic in our new circle of friends. She dressed in elaborate silks, and dainty lace gloves covered her exquisite hands. She walked with a red and white cane, for she was blind. Nevertheless, her past was as dramatic as any character's in James Clavell's "Nobel House" trilogy.

She said she had been married to a doctor who had kept her and their four children imprisoned for years on an island in the Pacific. She said her husband had beaten and sexually abused them all. She escaped to America, but was forced by her deranged, but influential husband to leave her children behind. After we became friends, she relished cooking gourmet dinners at my apartment and would invite a fascinating array of men and women. She would buy all the food and cook it herself, without any help from me or my daughters. After these gastronomic delights, our apartment would be permeated for days with strange and exotic odors. We didn't complain. On the contrary, we felt privileged to be exposed to the charm and mystery of a woman like Venus. Even more, we admired how this woman was able to get through pain and suffering far worse than most and yet have the courage to go on and create a new life for herself in a foreign land. We learned much from Venus.

Then there was Paul, the glamorous French race car driver who lived down the promenade from us. He dressed like an American cowboy, and he was a terrific storyteller. The girls and I loved to entice him into telling stories about his racing adventures. One evening the kids cornered him when he dropped by to say hello and begged, as usual, for a racing story. Paul settled down onto the couch, and the girls, Greg and I sat on the floor looking up in anticipation.

"It was the 1979 Paris to Dakar rally," he began in his throaty, French accent, "the world's most dangerous car race in one of the earth's hottest and most uninhabited regions. I was in my Renault 4 Sinpar race car," he said, crossing his long legs and swinging his expensive snakeskin boot up and down, "and drove for six thousand kilometers during seventeen days of grueling, gut-wrenching, dusty, dirty, windy roads that weaved from Paris to Algerie to Niger—the half-way point where many disasters occurred. A terrible storm stopped cars in their tracks, one driver died, while putting on his helmet and accidentally fell to the ground fracturing his skull, and then the Algerian government delayed us while they argued over their agreement to let the rally pass through their territory. We went through some of the poorest towns and villages of the Sahel, desert in Mauritania where many competitors got lost, through Mali, then to Senegal, a country of thirst, fear and mystery," he added with great drama. "And finally, the beautiful beaches of Dakar awaited the first race survivors, and I," he hesitated for a moment, "was one of them." Paul always left us breathless.

Christianna and Daniella both made life-long friends of their own at the Club. One of my favorites was Whitney, a high spirited, red-headed classmate of Daniella's who found a special place in my heart, not only because she had become Daniella's best friend and close to Christianna, too, but also because she had lost her adored, beautiful sister, Shonnon, earlier that year.

Shonnon had been a junior in high school the year she met a "wanna be" rock star who turned her on to drugs and a life on the streets in Hollywood. Her folks did everything to get her off the drugs and away from the ugly, degrading life she had fallen into. But they failed. Her addiction won. On a bright and sunny California morning, Shonnon was found dead of a heroine overdose lying on a bed alone in a dilapidated house on the lower east side of Sunset and Vine. Scared, her friends had fled the scene, not reporting her death until the following day.

My daughters could never take the place of Whitney's only sister, but they did offer the distraction of youthful, carefree friendship, and I could see that Whitney was beginning to come around and release some of her grief.

Daniella and Whitney soon became "double trouble" in our household. One evening, Whitney came over to spend the night with Daniella. I was going to dinner at Nick's, and since Daniella and Whitney said they had homework to do, Christianna decided to join me. The moment Christianna and I walked out the door, Daniella called downstairs to the Club's little sundry shop and said she was Mrs. Madruga and that she wanted a six-pack of Michelobe beer, a bag of Nachos and a hot Mexican bean dip sent up to Suite 245. When the delivery man arrived, he requested my signature to sign for the beer. Daniella apologized, saying that I was in the shower. She then yelled out to Whitney, who was in the bathroom with the shower going full blast, that the delivery man was at the door with the beer. Whitney, pretending to be me, shouted back to just sign the tab because it was a little inconvenient for her at the moment. The man handed Daniella the tab and she signed.

The girls played this trick more for the sake of doing it than for the beer, which they would leave in the refrigerator. Surprised to find it there, I would ask the girls where the beer had come from, and Daniella would say, off-handedly, "Oh, one of your friends probably left it." Whitney and Daniella delighted in creating such pranks and would merrily plot for days on how and when to execute their next practical joke.

Vivienne Lundquist, another new acquaintance, helped me rediscover an old love—horse-back-riding. Since leaving the ranch, I hadn't had any opportunity to ride until Vivienne and I found out over lunch one day that we shared a passion for horses. When I told her I used to barrel race before I lost my leg and had continued to ride after my surgery, but gave it up, because I couldn't tolerate the choppy trot of the quarter horse, she asked if I would like to go out to her ranch and experience the smoother ride of a Peruvian Paso. I 'd never heard of a Paso before, much less ridden one, but without any hesitation, I accepted.

It was a beautiful summer morning the day I headed for Vivienne's ranch. I got on the Pacific Coast Highway with the sting of the ocean breeze whipping against my face. I was feeling good; it had been a long time since I'd driven out of the concrete maze of the city and into the country, and an even longer interval since I'd been on a horse. I cut through the rugged Santa Monica mountains and drove north. I pulled onto to the freeway and followed the delicious aroma of mature orange groves which led me to Meadow Springs, a picture-perfect ranch nestled between gently rolling hills. I drove down a lane lined with whitewashed fences, and then I saw the Peruvians: golden palominos, hot-blooded stallions, elegant mares and fiery colts full of brio, galloping across lush, manicured pastures.

I parked alongside the ranch arena where I could see Vivienne, her long blond hair blowing in the wind, astride a powerful black stallion. She wore an embroidered white bolero shirt tucked into a pair of tight jeans, cinched with a sterling silver belt that accentuated her small waist. As she rode toward me, her arrogant horse arched his front legs high, out to the side and far forward, traveling like a conqueror. It was a majestic sight.

"Hi, Lenor, glad you could make it. Meet Antares. He's my grand champion, ranked number one in the U.S.," she proudly stated, patting his neck.

"My God, he's magnificent. What's all that flashy leg action about? I've never seen anything like it."

"It's a natural gait called 'termino'. The Peruvian is the smoothest riding horse on earth because of his unusual stride. Come on! Let's go for a ride."

At first, I was intimidated by the dynamic, high-stepping horse and panicky because I knew there could be no quick dismount when riding with a fake leg. But I wanted to ride again. A trainer offered his hand to help me get on a beautiful flaxen-maned mare, and with a little gentle prompting from Vivienne, I gripped the saddlehorn from the horse's right side and hoisted myself up by placing my good leg in the stirrup for support. I asked the trainer to pull my artificial leg over the horse's backside and place it into the left stirrup. As he struggled to position the leg, he apologized, thinking he was hurting me. "No, please," I laughed as I knocked on my leg. "I can't feel a thing."

After a few brief turns around the arena with Vivienne protectively at my side, I began to relax. I immediately fell in love with the Peruvian's smooth, lateral, four-beat step. As we rode out of the arena into shaded orchards, I felt exhilarated with the magic of independence that a horse always gives me as, he carries me over rocky roads, across creek-beds and up hills—through terrain that would be difficult, if not impossible, on foot.

Vivienne and I soon became good friends and riding partners. When she felt I was skilled enough on her Peruvians, she asked if I'd like to join the ranch's equestrian drill team called, "Easy Riders." I was honored and began practicing with the group once a week in precise show-stopping maneuvers called, "barrida."

One afternoon, as we rode over the cool, grassy fields of Meadow Springs, I mentioned to Viviene how different her ranch was from the dusty arenas where I used to ride in Tracy, competing in gymkhanna events at our local rodeos, banging my knees against rusty tin oil barrels while racing against the clock on my buckskin quarter-horse.

"Those years, horses and rodeos were a family affair," I told her. "Christianna and Daniella learned to barrel race on their Shetland ponies, and my husband team-roped with his best friend, Tony. We spent many hot, Sunday afternoons riding and competing with family and close friends." I paused, but then went on with my thought. "But there was one day of barrel racing I wish I'd missed," and as Vivienne and I rode our gentle, proud Peruvians through orange groves, I told her my story.

I was the last rider out for a final event at the annual Tracy Rodeo. Rodeo fans in make-shift grandstands and along worn fence posts cheered, as I rode into the arena. The intense heat of the afternoon sun beat against my back. Willy Nelson blared from the speakers, as my stocky little horse turned tightly into the first barrel and even tighter into the second. "One more barrel to go," I thought with growing excitement, "and I'll be home free with a first place ribbon." I bore down on the third and last barrel at high speed, guiding my horse through his cycle. As we came out of the spin for the accelerated race to the finish line, I felt my horse lose his footing in the soft dirt and, as if in slow motion, begin to fall. With a violent thud, my horse landed on my left side, pinning me under 1000 pounds of horseflesh. The saddle-horn rammed into my pelvis with excruciating pain. For weeks, the entire left side of my body was sore and discolored with bruising. It was difficult to walk, easier to ride. The injury healed and never bothered me again, but two years later, in the exact area of the wound, I found the cancerous lump that changed my life forever. When I asked the doctors if the fall had anything to do with the tumor, they said they didn't know, but if they did, they could cure a lot of cancer.

I rode with Vivienne's drill team for about a year and on New Year's day of 1983 we rode in the Rose Bowl Parade in Pasadena, California. Christianna and Daniella tried to get into the act, too, by running as fast as they could down Colorado Boulevard in a vain attempt to keep up with our riding group. As we passed the grandstand, it was announced that our horses wore "the look of eagles!"

Life was good for me now—I was enjoying former pleasures again; my girls were thriving; the pain of divorce was shoved into a drawer; I had a coterie of fascinating friends and then, to make things complete, I had a whirlwind romance.

One day I stepped into the Club's elevator and ran into an old acquaintance whom I had met, while I was still married to Joseph, at a book signing in Los Angeles. His name was Didder Hoelft and he was an international real estate investor. At the signing, he had bought one of my books for his son, who was battling cancer. Later, Didder spent the evening with me and my traveling companion, Dianne, talking and sipping brandy in the hotel bar.

After spending a very nice evening, Dianne and I excused ourselves, mentioning I had to be up early for a television appearance.

Now when I saw Didder, I grinned broadly, partly because I was so glad to see him but partly because I remembered at once the day after that evening we sat up drinking brandy. Late-night brandy had been enjoyable, but I had paid for it the next morning. I wasn't hung over—I didn't think; quite the contrary. If fact, I felt euphoric, anticipating my first major television appearance, as Dianne and I slid into the luxurious backseat of the long white limousine the studio had sent, complete with a chauffeur clad in full uniform to take us to West Hollywood for the television show.

As we drove toward Hollywood, I remember enjoying the attention of all the other drivers and passengers who were craning their necks to see who was in the glamorous car (I even rolled down my window to give them the "thumbs up!"). But as the car maneuvered through the back streets to avoid the crowded morning freeways, I suddenly began to feel sick. My stomach churned. Dizziness and nausea swept over me. At first I thought I was nervous over the show, and then, guiltily, I remembered last night's brandy. As my head began to spin, the limo seemed to grow in size, increasing its length, as it gobbled up each block. It felt like I was been transported to the studio by a giant serpent.

"Dianne," I hoarsely whispered, "I'm going to throw up."

"Oh no, you can't throw up, not in here!" And then she saw my sick expression. "You are going to throw up, but where for God's sake?"

"Paul, could you please pull the car over to the side of the road" I managed to ask, genteelly.

"Yes, Mrs. Madruga, is there anything wrong?"

"I think," I gulped, "I'm going to be sick. My first television show… you understand, nerves…"

Paul frantically edged the monstrous car over to a curb. He shot out the driver's seat and rushed over to open the door. "May I assist you?" he asked, while extending a meticulous white-gloved hand.

I stepped out of the car with as much decorum as I could muster. Then I casually pulled my long hair away from my face, gracefully untied the bow at my neck, tossed the ties over my shoulders, seized the chauffeur's hand, and proceeded to puke all over the side of his limousine. With the flare of a fan dancer, Paul whisked from his breast pocket a spotless white linen handkerchief. Daintily, I dabbed at the corners of my mouth and then handed it back to him. "Thank you, Paul," I said graciously. Dianne swears I acted as if I'd just finished afternoon tea.

When I got back into the car, I felt much better but was too concerned about making it through the television show to appreciate the humor of the situation. Paul drove us to the backstage door of the studio and said he would pick us up after the show. "In the meantime," he said, "I think I'll take the car through the car wash."

And now, four years later, Didder and I accidentally were meeting again. He had arrived that morning from his home in Bad Hamburg, Germany and was in town on business. I invited him to my apartment. We sat on the balcony with the afternoon sun bright against the glossy boats in the harbor, and talked about the intervening years since we had last seen each other. He asked what I was doing at the Club again, and I briefly explained about my divorce. I asked him about his son.

"My son died," he responded softly. "I couldn't help him."

I was not shocked by his son's death, as I had known from our last conversation that his condition was terminal. But I was saddened, not only by the death of a child, but for a father who felt he had failed to save his only son.

During the next two weeks, Didder and I spent every evening together, and I became more and more attracted to this tall, wiry, thirty-six-year-old, Warren Beatty look-alike with a whimsical smile. I delighted in his accent and admired the way he knew as much about our history and culture, as he knew about his own. I even liked the way he smoked a cigarette, with his index finger curled around the Gauloise brand that Europeans seemed to prefer. I'd never met anyone other than Joseph who had such a riveting effect on me.

The night before his departure for London, we went dancing atop the Beverly Hills Wilshire Hotel. He drew me to him and held me close, and we began to dance, slowly at first, so we could get the feel, the balance. I was able to follow his every step with my artificial leg. His arms held me tight, and we danced in the moment as if we were one. After several dances, Didder looked at me and whispered, "Let's go."

We went back to the Club, and he led me directly to his room. "But Didder," I protested, "you know I have to be up early to get the girls off to school."

"I want to make love to you," he said simply.

"But Didder, I don't know…"

He offered me a glass of mineral water, which didn't surprise me, because I knew he wasn't much of a drinker.

"No, no thank you…yes, I mean, yes, thank you," I said stalling for time.

"Please, Lenor," he said calmly," sit down and relax."

The only place to sit was on the bed. I sat down on the edge. As he handed me the glass of water, he held my eyes with a soulful look and lightly stroked my cheek. Nervous, I started talking fast, nonsensical. He wasn't listening. He cupped my face in his hands and kissed me. In spite of my trepidation, I found myself responding, willingly entering his embrace. My God, it had been such a long time since I'd been touched, kissed or appreciated in that way.

Gently he eased me down onto the bed—no small feat considering the pounds of metal strapped around my hips. I was unsure of myself. How could Didder possibly find me sexy with my body bound in a huge, cumbersome prop that made my movements more robotic then graceful? I wasn't used to making love burdened with heavy hardware on. With

Joseph, I could always slip into something more comfortable—meaning get out of my leg, bathe and don a negligee.

As Didder continued to kiss me, I could feel his hands slowly glide down my back. My body softened, then tensed as I realized how close he was to the stiff, plastic brace. "If his hands roam any further", I thought in nervous amusement, "he risks getting his fingers caught."

"This is ridiculous," I said to myself as I tried to get the momentum to sit back up again. It wasn't that I didn't want to make love to Didder, but that I was afraid of the unknown factors: how to deal with the brace, how to be appealing under these conditions, how to proceed without dispelling the precious romantic mood, and how it would be to have sex with my disability with a man other than my husband."

"It doesn't matter," he murmured as he softly kissed my eyelids, the tip of my nose, my lips and down to the soft indentation of my neck.

A decision had to be made. I would either stay and make love to this man or leave. The more he gently touched me, the less I wavered. This man was beginning to kindle more than just my ego. His natural acceptance of me, and our mutual passion for each other soon outweighed any thoughts of embarrassment or guilt.

However, I had a problem—how to slip into something more comfortable without being noticed. I excused myself and went straight to the bathroom and locked the door. "Now what? Oh, God, how did I get myself into this situation? Too late now, girl, you've made your decision."

Filled with trepidation, I slowly unbuckled and removed the leg. My first thought was how I was going to move, get around without my leg on and with no crutches. And then came the paralyzing fear of wondering what Didder would think once he saw me with only one leg. Would he find me repulsive? Unbalanced? Would I be rejected? I decided Didder could only find me unsightly if I found myself to be. I did not. I was clear on that.

My next concern was where to put the leg? Ah ha, the shower. As I set the leg against the tile, I couldn't avoid smiling at the thought of the expression Didder would have on his face if he opened the curtain and saw the solitary leg, dressed in its evening finery, leaning against the wall. After I closed the curtain, I felt like I was saying good-bye to a part of me and hello to a whole new venture.

I pulled a bath towel off the rack and covered myself. I hopped over to the door and cautiously opened it.

"May I assist you?" Didder gallantly offered.

"Yes, please," I said with the palms of my hands out-stretched, indicating I had no other way to get to him. Without another word, he scooped me up into his arms and carried me to bed.

That night I dove into uncharted waters, not knowing if the temperature would be cold or inviting. I braved it and completely lost myself in warm, passionate caresses. As our love-making progressed, it was obvious to me from Didder's attentions and my reactions that I was still sensuous, desirable and attractive, capable of exciting men and being satisfied myself as well. At that moment, I knew I was undiminished and every bit the woman I'd always been.

The next morning, the sun rose glorious and bright through my bedroom window. I felt wonderful, fulfilled. I relived every moment of our evening together, Didder's smell, his kiss, his maleness. I had no illusions about falling in love or sharing a future life with Didder. I just wanted to love and be loved, if only for one night, something I hadn't experienced for a very long time. And to know that even with my amputation, I could still attract a man like Didder was an important turning point for me. Ecstatic, I now had a new view of myself and my expectations for the future.

Chapter 7
Some Tough Years

After Didder's departure for London, I was left with only romantic memories of our time together. I sometimes wondered if I'd ever find another man who could make me feel normal and beautiful again. I had slipped into this melancholy mood late one evening when there was a knock at my door.

It was the hotel bellhop. He handed me a note. "Have a nice evening," he said smiling, as he walked away.

I had an ominous feeling about the note. Nervous, I poured a brandy and walked out on the terrace. I looked out over the tranquil harbor. Dim lights softly glowed from boat cabins and I could hear the sound of expensive boats. Bound to their moorings, they rocked and creaked, struggling to free themselves from their ties. It was a typical harbor scene that had always brought me peace and comfort. Until this night.

I opened the note.

"This is an eviction notice. You have one week to leave the premises..." I could read no further.

Oh God, please, no. What was I going to do? Where would I go, and what about the girls? I knew this day was inevitable, but why now, when everything seemed to be coming together? Too tired and upset to think any more of the scrap of paper still clutched in my hand, I savored one last lingering glance at the harbor lights, went to my room, and crawled into bed.

The next morning, the threatening note still heavy on my mind, I slowly tumbled out of bed. Groggily, I went into the bathroom and splashed cold water on my face. I made a pot of coffee, woke up the girls and asked them to join me on the terrace. Sensing something was wrong, they followed me out to the deck and fell quiet, waiting for me to speak.

Their reaction to my grim news surprised me. "It's okay, mom. We always felt this was only temporary, anyway. It never really felt like home, not *our* home."

I called Nick. He calmly said that maybe it was for the best, since Sam, the president, had recently left the Club. And, since he knew there was no way I could come up with the huge sum I already owed the Club, maybe it wasn't such a bad idea to get out on my own, find a job that would pay for our living expenses, and with what was left, pay a little back to the Club each month.

Nick's words motivated me. Why not move on? It *was* time. The girls were happy anticipating living somewhere else, so maybe leaving Marina Del Rey wasn't the end of the world. With no other option, my practical side kicked in and I immediately prepared to leave the Club.

Nick, hoping he hadn't hurt my feelings with his blunt assessment, came over that afternoon. The four of us sat down and discussed alternatives to living in Marina del Rey. The girls brought up the idea of moving to Santa Cruz, the seaside community in northern California where we used to holiday as a family.

"All our friends vacation there in summer," Daniella said with growing excitement. "And," Christianna, added, "Tracy's only two hours away. We could see dad and grandma more often."

Since I couldn't think of anywhere else to move, it was decided. We'd go to Santa Cruz.

With no extra money on hand, I called my father and asked if he would co-sign on a lease for us. He agreed. I then called Cathy Zupan, my intrepid traveling companion of a few years back who lived near Santa Cruz. I asked if she knew of any jobs I might be qualifed for in the area. Not surprised by my question, as we'd kept in close touch since our last trip together, she said, "Just get here, Lenor. You can work with me selling advertising."

So, three years after moving to the Club, in March of 1985, the girls and I packed my little sports car with our few personal belongings and, once again, set out on another journey.

My dear father was waiting at the local real estate office when we arrived in Santa Cruz. That very day we found a small, furnished, nondescript house in La Selva Beach near Santa Cruz, signed the lease and moved in. Christianna and Daniella were happy to be in a place that held fond childhood memories for them. "Remember the beach houses we used to rent here, Mom?" Christianna said as she looked out the window. "With Tony and Ann, and Anthony and Gloria and all their kids? How we couldn't wait to leave hot, old Tracy?"

"Yeah," said Daniella, "and go to the beach and swim, build sand castles, roast marshmallows and sing around bonfires at night? And how exciting it was when Dad would buzz us in his rented plane, and then we'd all pile in the car and go pick him up? You remember, Mom?"

I remembered, but that's not what I was feeling. I felt at loose ends. I wasn't a contented housewife on holiday; I was a divorcee with two teenage daughters and in desperate need of a job. I didn't know anyone in Santa Cruz, and, after the last few years of enjoying a semblance of success, suddenly I was a *nobody*. I had the additional worry of Santa Cruz's notorious drug reputation—that drugs were as available as candy. I feared for my girls.

After I got Christianna and Daniella settled into local schools, I called Cathy about the job she had mentioned. It had sounded attractive when I first heard the word "advertising," but when I talked to Cathy on the phone and she explained further, it didn't have quite the allure.

"You'll be paid only on commission; your area will include two counties—meaning you'll be driving a lot. And, one more thing," she added, "you'll have to pay your own expenses."

Cathy sympathized when she heard my disappointment. "I know, I know, it's hard work, and you have a little cash flow problem. But the job will pay the bills."

Cathy was right. I couldn't be picky. Compelled to put a roof over my children's' heads and food on the table I initiated my first masquerade. I was good at disguise and managed to look and sound convincing in my trumped up role as an "advertising executive." My only drawback was walking. In those days, vanity dictated I wear two-inch heels. For a radical amputee, this was not a good choice, especially when I sometimes had to walk entire city blocks searching for addresses. And I'd do this carrying— sometimes dragging—my heavy briefcase while negotiating curbs and steep inclines. I worried my knee would not lock up as it should when in a slant position. When it rained, I feared slippery sidewalks or, worse, the wet tile entrances of clients' offices.

As I trekked in and out of buildings, I prayed for strength to get me through each day. Soon, I mastered the obstacles that blocked my way and began to sell ads with relative ease. Finally, I was able to squeeze out enough on commissions to live and to pay back some of my debt to the Marina Beach Club. Yet, my efforts selling unwanted advertising lasted only a few months. I started having problems with wear and tear on my artificial leg. I couldn't risk it giving out, so my beat as an advertising executive was short lived.

About this time, I received a call from a close friend of Joseph's and mine who, since our divorce, had made repeated efforts to get us back together. "You must come to Tracy and see Joseph," he said to me. He was concerned because he said Joseph was very depressed, spending too much time alone in the house with the shades drawn. "Say you'll come," he begged, "I know Joseph still loves you."

For a second, my heart leaped, but then stopped cold. No, Joseph didn't love me. In my mind, he had placed no worth, no value on our marriage. His choice to end it had destroyed a family. And for what? Joseph's and Brenda's relationship ended a year after she moved into our home. No, I wouldn't be traveling to Tracy.

Over the past few years I had built-up great resentment toward Joseph. Only when I was able to forgive him and myself for whatever went terribly wrong in what I considered to be a beautiful marriage, was I able to finally shake the ugly bitterness. But the memory of what we once had, never died.

After I quit the sales job, I signed on with Kelly Girls, a temporary work service, hoping that I could select jobs that wouldn't include arduous walking. Afraid my disability might rob me of an assignment, I never mentioned that I was an amputee. I never brought up the fact that I was an author, either. I couldn't risk potential employers thinking I was an overqualified applicant. So I forced myself to go out and masquerade at jobs for which I was woefully unqualified.

First, I talked my way into a two week position as secretary to the editor of the *Herald Tribune* in Monterey which meant an hour's drive from home, an eight hour shift and a lot of getting up and down from my desk and walking to and from the editor's office.

"What secretarial skills do you have?" the editor asked, during my first interview.

"Oh, many," I responded glibly, "most all."

I got the job and then had to play out the role. I surprised myself by handling most of the secretarial duties, except for shorthand. When the editor called me into his office for dictation, I'd pretend to understand his thick Cockney accent and frantically scribbled down everything he said. As soon as he finished talking, I'd charge back to my desk and type as fast as I could, relying only on my notes and memory. One afternoon, looking puzzled after reading one of his letters, he said, "Lenor, did I dictate this…?"

"Oh, I'm sorry. I probably mixed it up with the other letter, or perhaps the other one…?" My excuse was feeble. I was out the door that afternoon.

I played switchboard operator for a brokerage house for about three months. This job wasn't physically difficult, only boring. When I got fed up answering the same message in the same way each day, I drew on my theatrical background and started answering the phone in various Italian, French and Irish accents. It put a little pizzazz into my role, and I began to have fun with the monotonous job, until the boss fired me because he said he was tired of hearing: "Another *new* operator, George?"

So it was on to my next masquerade as a computer operator in the basement of a depressing, gray, cinderblock Social Security building. After a week of just trying to figure out how to run the machine, I was rescued by my French agent saying that my publisher in Holland wanted me there for the promotion of the Dutch edition of my book. I dropped everything and prepared for my trip to Holland.

After a year of pretending to be someone I was not and working at jobs that meant nothing to me—except monetarily—I was suddenly a *somebody* again, transported from Kelly Girl in Santa Cruz to author in Amsterdam. And for two weeks I was grateful not to have to mask who I was, to work authentically at what I knew and loved. When I arrived, I called my former roommate, Judy Graves, who was living in Germany, and asked if she could join me at the Pulitzer Hotel. Judy had lost her breast to cancer the same year I had lost my leg. We hadn't seen each other since then.

With Judy at my side, my days began with interviews, usually in quaint pubs, and then I went to radio and television appearances. Judy and I would cap off the evenings talking into the night sharing the wondrous and difficult years that had passed between us. Judy told me that she had been cured of cancer after her left breast had been removed.

"Hey, I never had great breasts anyway," Judy said. "My legs were my best asset."

"And my breasts were mine," I laughed.

The next day my editor arranged for me to meet with a Dutch beauty queen who, after being crowned the most beautiful girl in Holland, discovered she had cancer. To save her life, doctors had amputated her left leg and hip. She was only twenty-one years old.

We met in my suite at the hotel. Anneke came in the door on crutches with her family and her fiancé. Questions flew and eyes followed my every step. After answering most of the concerns of her family, Anneke asked if she could speak to me alone.

We went into the other room. "May I see how you put your leg on and...," Anneke hesitated, "how you take it off?"

"Sure," I said, as I unstrapped and slipped my leg off. I then sat down on a chair and stood the leg beside me. Curious, Anneke stared at it, then cautiously touched it. She asked if the thing that strapped around my hips hurt when I wore it.

I told her it could hurt if I didn't protect my skin from the bucket's hard surface. I then held up the thick, sock-like undergarment I wore—I didn't have the heart, at that moment, to tell her that silk bikini panties would no longer fit into her wardrobe if she wore an artificial leg. Then I showed her how I take my nylons off and on and how I camouflage the bulk of the phony leg with the right clothing.

"You see, it's possible to wear an artificial leg," I said, as I put my leg back on, "and you can still look normal, attractive."

If Anneke was disturbed, she didn't let on.

"Before tonight," Anneke said, holding back her tears, " I thought my life was over. That I would never walk again. Now, I know I can do it," she said, trying to compose herself. " I will walk again."

That same week, I met with her doctors and prosthetists. They said they were astounded to see a person with such an overwhelming amputation wear a limb and walk. They contacted my prothetist in the States and with his collaboration, succeeded in building Anneke a leg. Later, I received pictures of Anneke, still a "beauty queen," walking down the aisle on her wedding day.

On Judy's final afternoon in Amsterdam, I accompanied her to the train station. As I stood on the platform waving, I could see her face pressed against the window as the train departed. We wouldn't see each other again for many years.

After my tour of Holland and precious time shared with Judy, and meeting Anneke, I left for California. It was a letdown to be back in Santa Cruz, where I had to don a false persona again. I questioned my life's purpose. Other than being a mother to my girls, how was I making a difference in the world? And what about my covenant with god? My promessa? I couldn't let myself fall into that snare of self-pity. I had to go on.

My days of driving long distances and working at droll jobs at Kelly Girls took a turn for the better when I met Trey Scott, the son of producer Tim Scott, who had been trying to arouse interest in a television project on my book for the past year. Trey reminded me of my older brother, Ernie, with his eager and exuberant personality. He was working at a local CBS affiliate, and, after we met, we began discussing the possibility of starting up our own television production company.

Since going through cancer and amputation, I had searched for ways to bring new meaning and direction to others who had experienced a life altered by fate. And, I had often thought, what better way to fulfill that promise than through the medium of television? Trey's goal had always been to produce television shows that offered "entertainment with integrity." Together, we hoped to accomplish both our missions by producing half-hour magazine talk shows that focused on people who had overcome major life set-backs.

At last, I was back to working at something which felt meaningful to me. During the next year, Trey and I tapped into family, friends and foes to buy shares into our production company, which we formed with the assistance of a mutual friend. Trey continued to work at CBS and I stayed at Kelly Girls, but we worked into the night putting together proposals, newsletters and mailers and calling on prospective shareholders. It became a family affair with the girls' pitching in stuffing envelopes, answering the phone and taking messages. After twelve months of intense and nerve-wracking pitching, cajoling and begging potential investors, we finally quit our day jobs, pooled our talents and wrote our first television show, *Stepping Into Life*.

After completing a rough script, written long-hand at my kitchen table, we then selected, from the many letters I'd received over the years, guests who we thought would fit into the format which we composed. We came up with three provocative stories: the inspirational life of Milan Tiff, a man who had defied a crippling disease and became a world class athlete; Dr. Wilbur, a man who was considered to be a maverick in the medical field because of his unconventional approach to treating children with cancer; and Dr. Muriel James, the best-selling author of *Born to Win* (who just happened to be my stepmother of thirty years.) Muriel was an authority on the dynamics of well-being and offered sound advice on how people could take charge of their lives in difficult times.

Trey hand-picked, from his talented circle of family and friends, a professional television crew to shoot the pilot show which I hosted and he directed. After filming the introduction and the segments—with the girls holding up the cue cards they had written—we closed with me riding a grand Peruvian Paso at Paharo Beach. Trey filmed this final shot hanging, precariously, out of the window of a small airplane while I tried, in vain, to control my horse from spooking, as the plane flew directly overhead. With great satisfaction, Trey captured the scene he wanted—me on an excited, powerful horse galloping over the dunes at Paharo Beach mirroring the image of a person moving on—escaping the confines of disability.

With our production finished and the show "in the can," Trey and I popped our wares into the backseat of my car and headed south down the freeway singing, "Hollywood, Hollywood!"

In Los Angeles we stayed at Al and Robbie's on their couch and guest bed. Too excited to sleep, Trey and I took off early in the morning and drove to the first of many television studios. Once there, we knocked on doors, talked to receptionists and secretaries. At the second studio, we got lucky and briefly met with a major TV producer. As soon as we got in the door, Trey slipped our video into the VCR and as *Stepping Into Life* began to play, we explained why our pilot would be an attractive and important addition to their programming.

The producer liked the refreshing and original look of the project and its message.

"I'll review it with our people," he said. "I'll get back to you."

As time went on, we got this same answer from other producers—so we hammered on.

Meeting and talking with these high-profile TV executives was encouraging, yet our attempts to convince them to understand that we had a worthwhile project was hard. Getting in and out of the car, re-adjusting my leg and walking the distances (thankful, every step of the way, for Trey's strong arm) was fatiguing. We grew disappointed when we realized that the market we had chosen to enter was bigger and more difficult to break into than we had ever imagined. Still, over the next year, Trey and I pushed on, traveling and knocking on more doors while at the same time juggling our own personal lives.

Our pilot was screened in many cities throughout the country. But alas, we finally ran out of money. Without funds, we could no longer travel and continue to pitch our show. In the end, we were just a small independent company trying to compete with the huge television networks. Whether it was due to lack of timing, my non-celebrity status or not the right contacts, the project never got off the ground.

Trey and I were forced to abandon our dream. We were spent, dejected. Even more, we felt that we had let down our faithful investors, though we had done everything humanly possible to sell the show. But in the end, we felt proud that we were able to form a company, produce a television pilot and take it on the road. We had embarked on an adventure that came from our hearts, capturing the imagination of our family, friends and supporters and we had seen it through.

"If we don't take risks," Trey said, after the demise of our small company, "then we fail. If we don't have our fantasies, then we only have the starkness of our realities. Dreams are the child force that sparks hope and innocence. Dreams give meaning to our existence."

Like Trey, I, too, enjoyed risk taking. I knew there would be another day, another dream. But until then, it was back to work at Kelly Girls, and for Trey, teaching at a local high school.

My next assignment at Kelly Girls, was the unlikely job of bill collector. The irony of this job was inescapable—me pressuring other people to pay their bills when I could barely make my own phone payment each month. Instead of making people feel worthwhile, which I took pleasure in, I was making them miserable with my insistent demands to pay their bills. I was grateful when the job was over.

For a while, I pretended to be matchmaker in a Millionaires Singles Club for people who hoped to find wealthy mates…but for a hefty price. I quit when I found out the Club was just a scam with no millionaires, just a lot of lonely people hoping to get lucky and find a rich partner.

My life was not only a hodgepodge of jobs—but it was a lonely life, too. If it hadn't been for my daughters and the need to care for them, worry about them, and be there for them, I don't know how I would have fared. Christianna and Daniella were my impetus to carry on, no matter what.

Fortunately, the girls loved Santa Cruz—going so far as to change their appearances just to fit in. Daniella dropped her L.A. "new wave" look and switched to "hippie" tie-dyed garments, flowers in her hair and a peace sign painted on her left shoulder. Christianna liked the "surfer" girl look—501 jeans, tee-shirts covered with surfing logos and long straight, bleached hair. I worried how far they might go to fit in to the free-spirited scene that was prevalent in Santa Cruz. Would it lead to drugs, drinking, partying, or random sex that were common in this innocent-looking, picture-perfect coastal town? I prayed my girls were smarter than that.

As they headed for school each morning, I'd watch them walk down the sandy beach path together, and as they disappeared around the bend, I'd smile at their striking contrasts. It had always been so, even before their recent "new look" changes. In the past, everyone used to call Daniella "little Lenor," because she looked so similar to me with her blue eyes, dark hair and skin.

"Daniella might look like mom," Christianna, my fair-haired blond, would respond. "but I act like her."

They may have looked and acted differently, but when it came to their mother, their hearts were in the same place. I used to call them "Mommy's little legs," because whenever I'd run up against difficult tasks, I'd call on them for help. In our old home in Tracy, up and down the stairs their little legs would run as they fetched my lipstick or searched for my purse. At the grocery store, they'd run ahead of me and grab whatever I needed, then run back and find me somewhere between the aisles slowly pushing my cart. With impish looks on their faces, they'd toss cans of beans, bags of vegetables or fruit in my direction, sometimes landing their mark, sometimes not. It didn't matter. The girls were helping do an everyday, simple chore that would have been fatiguing for me on my own.

Through the years, my appreciation for them has grown even deeper.

Our first summer in Santa Cruz Daniella, at only fourteen, met her future husband, Elliott Crowder, Jr. Elliott, three years older than Daniella, was a typical Santa Cruz "surfer"—tall and narrow with long blond hair and a sweet, laid-back attitude. His dad, whom we all called "Big E," because of his lanky, 6'5" frame, was a pilot instructor at the local airport. Elliott was raised by Big E and shared a close relationship with him. Before going to California, they had sailed the South Pacific on a 30-foot schooner for two years, lived off the land in the wilds of Vermont and criss-crossed America in a beat up VW bus. They finally settled in La Selva Beach, a year before we arrived. I liked little Elliott a lot, and hoped that he would be a good influence on Daniella. Soon, Elliott introduced the girls to all his close buddies.

They were a group of surfers who, with their surfboards cradled under their arms, their hair streaked by the bright summer sun, their bodies lithe but taut, would catch the waves each day down at Manressa Beach. They were athletic boys with competitive, yet polite personalities. I felt comfortable when they were around the girls.

Big E and I became surrogate dad and mom to our respective children, the surfer boys and many of their siblings. I'd feed them and Big E would keep tabs on them during week-end bonfires at the beach. That first summer, he would stand up on the bluff resting on his classic 1946 BMW motorcycle looking out over the Pacific—fooling no one as he kept one eye on the party below.

The years I spent as a farm wife had prepared me to cook *big*. So I never minded when Elliott, his surfer buddies and other new friends of the girls scrambled around our dinner table in the evening, sitting on mix-matched chairs, all sharing from a huge pot of chili. The kids were lively and interesting, and they earned their keep, too. Elliott shopped for me, Ryo mopped my floors, Chris vacuumed, Lee was my mechanic and Kirk, the oldest of the boys at twenty, was my bartender. After a hard day at work, Kirk, unfailingly, would have a chilled glass of white wine poured for me the moment I walked through the door.

I could continue working the demanding, and sometimes demeaning jobs, I took on at Kelly Girls, because I looked forward to coming home to the girls and their new friends—all of us eating together and enjoying each other's company. It was a critical time in these teenagers' lives. Many seldom saw their parents, who left early in the morning, usually commuting over the hill to San Jose to work, not getting home until late and rarely sharing meals together. These kids often came to me with their problems and I tried to be of help.

My phone may not have been ringing off the hook with exciting invitations to parties, and I wasn't a star in Paris, but I was an appreciated mother doing her best to support and keep her family together. Indeed, I was a *somebody*, after all.

But soon, everything changed in our house.

Two years after moving to La Selva Beach I was forced to rent out one of our back bedrooms to help pay the rent. After interviewing several candidates, I selected Steve, a twenty-five-year-old young man from Ohio, who seemed the perfect gentleman, perfect roommate. The only disconcerting thing about Steve was the prominent dark ink-like circles that pooled under his eyes. Since he was of Russian descent, I figured it had something to with his heritage.

Not so. Steve was a drug addict, snorting cocaine mornings in his bedroom, before going to work, at work, and again when he got home. Unbeknownst to me or Big E, and under the tutelage of Steve, the girls and their friends were soon experimenting with all kinds of drugs, kindly supplied by Steve. I never caught my daughters because they usually got high after school down at the beach or at friends' houses and when they'd get home they'd go straight to their rooms avoiding me so I wouldn't see them in their altered states.

After a while, I began to wonder why they were withdrawing from family life, not appreciating my "big" cooking anymore and sleeping a lot. And I wondered why the other teenagers weren't hanging around anymore. Weary from too many hours of driving and working, I let the situation slide. I assumed they were all just going through some teenage stage.

Everything came to a head late one night when I heard weird noises coming from the kitchen. I got up to see what was going on, and as I crutched down the hallway I could hear Steve whispering to someone and the sound of a hair dryer.

"Steve, what are you doing? And who's this?" I asked, pointing at the stranger behind the kitchen sink. "What are you doing with the hair dryer on?"

Steve didn't say a word. He just stared at me with those strange eyes.

And then I saw what looked to me like newspaper comic strips spread across the counter tops. "What's this?" I asked, totally mystified. When I got my answer, I was appalled. They were making hits of acid under my nose, in my house, in a family neighborhood in La Selva Beach.

Livid, I kicked Steve and his friend out. Then and there, I woke up the girls and hustled them into the living room and demanded to know what had been going on.

"I can't believe this!" I screamed. "Did you know what Steve was doing? If you did, why didn't you tell me? My god, I've never been so shocked in my life," I said, shaking, as I leaned on my crutches to steady myself. "And you girls. Have you been doing drugs?" I eyed them with ferocity. "I want the truth NOW! About EVERYTHING!"

Through tears and sorrowful apologies, the girls came clean, admitting that Steve had been giving them and their friends all kinds of drugs "just to try." But things had been getting out of hand lately, they said, and they were getting paranoid about everything—just taking the bus made them edgy because they were afraid someone could tell they were on drugs. They said they were petrified that I'd find out.

At first, all I could show was disbelief. How could I have been so stupid? Why didn't I notice? And I felt terrible guilt at providing the perfect trap by bringing a drug addict into our home. Drugs, the thing I dreaded most about Santa Cruz, had come home to roost—but not for long. I would never accept drugs or lies in our home.

During the next year, I was constantly worried, even though the girls had promised that they would never again do drugs. They said they felt horrible about the whole thing and regretted, more than anything, that they had betrayed my trust. They wanted it back.

Since I was gone during the day Monday through Friday, continuing to work at various temporary jobs, the opportunity for them to tamper with drugs was ever-present. And I feared that their friends might still be on drugs. With that kind of peer pressure I knew anything could happen. All I could do was try to get them to communicate with me and talk openly about anything and everything.

Slowly, the girls began letting me in on their lives more than ever before. They talked about school (Daniella, not surprisingly, hated it), boyfriends (Christianna played the field, but Daniella was still madly in love with Elliott), sex (they both were experimenting, so we talked of disease, protection and how it would be nice to be in love with a partner before having sex) and on and on. I prayed we were making progress.

After living a tough two years in La Selva Beach, our lease was up, and we moved again. A small house in Rio Del Mar, another beach front community, was our next home. The girls were in school and off drugs—their friends, too, were clean and sober and back in the folds of our family.

With the drug experience behind us, the kids looked forward to coming over to our house again to have dinner or just to be together. Daniella, determined to stay healthy, became a vegetarian and took over the household cooking. We didn't have a lot of money, so our menu was limited to things like steamed fresh vegetables and rice, topped off with the cheese my mom used to get in huge blocks from the social security office and send to us. Christianna, or whoever else was at hand, would do the dishes. After dinner, we'd sit on the floor around our used TV set that had a tiny screen and watch movies or just talk. We felt like one big family again. And I understood, more than ever, the importance of having your children and their friends around you, seeing their faces, talking to them, listening to them—hearing them.

At this time, Christianna was a senior at Aptos High and doing well scholastically. She was involved in both the Drama and French Clubs and enjoyed many of the after school social activities.

Daniella, on the other hand, wasn't keen on high school at all. She wasn't into football games, cheerleading or any of the other preppy things the school had to offer. She was unhappy. Her grades fell below average. She begged me to let her go to a nearby alternative school where she could maybe find her niche. Finally, I agreed and after years of trying to ditch school, Daniella suddenly couldn't wait to go to school and she excelled. She became editor of the school paper and president of her class, and began working after school with the mentally challenged, which became a life-long passion. She liked working with young developmentally disabled, because, she said, "they're so innocent, like babies who need to be taken care of. They need to be protected and watched out for. They need a voice." (I remember thinking how sweet and true that was.)

The most important thing in my life was the knowledge that Christianna and Daniella were doing well. With that in place, I was set free to focus on my own life which, I suddenly realized, didn't have much going for it. At least not a social life. Since moving to Santa Cruz the only men I'd met, other then Trey, were drifters, aged surfers or old hippies trying to hang on to the 60's life-style of slovenliness, excessive drink and drugs—not what I was interested in. In this atmosphere, I wondered if I would ever find a satisfying social life, or love, again.

Then Elias Vernikos came into my life. We met in Carmel, California through a real estate agent I was working for as a receptionist. The moment we were introduced, I was attracted to this man. Elias was dark, tall, handsome, extremely intelligent and, for toppers, the godson of Aristotle Onassis. After we started dating, Elias captivated me with fascinating stories of his youth where he spent holidays with his godfather, Aristotle, his exquisite first wife, Tina, and their children cruising the Greek Isles on Aristotle's yacht, the *Christina*. After seven years of being unmarried and after Didder, I found Elias to be the most charming and interesting date yet.

We spent week-ends together snooping around fishing villages along the Monterey coast, we ate fresh oysters, clams and lobsters in little clapboard weathered fish houses that sat side-by-side on piers jetting out into the shark-infested northern California waters. We drank robust red wines, while I sat glued to my wobbly wooden seat, enthralled with Elias's vivid stories of his relatives, the Onassis's and the Starvos's families. Elias liked to be around harbors, because it brought back memories of childhood summers with his dad who owned a fleet of tug boats in Greece.

I was proud to introduce Elias to my family and friends. I would have liked to fall in love with him, but I was looking for the love that I had felt with Joseph, and it just didn't happen. Friends would say, "Lenor, you experienced great love once; it doesn't often come again." If that were so, I thought, then I would be spending the rest of my days alone.

After many months of enjoying time with Elias, he returned to Greece and I was back to square one—no man and little social life. Disappointed that our relationship hadn't turned into love, for either of us, another low point set in.

If anyone could lift my spirits it was my sister, Diane. The weekend after Elias left, the girls and I scraped together gas money, and on Friday afternoon, headed up to Diane's ranch in the foothills of the Sierra Mountains. Diane, a red-headed beauty with a bubbly personality was divorced with two teen daughters of her own and dealing with some of the same problems I had dealt with. But she was living her dream of raising and boarding horses on her ranch.

LouAnn, a knock-out, long-legged blond, an old friend from Tracy, joined us that week-end with her teenage son and daughter. LouAnn was living her dream, too, designing (in her basement) leather fashions for some of America's top country singers.

Saturday morning we woke to the sounds of roosters crowing, dogs barking, peacocks shrilling. Diane appeared in her ridiculous Chinese straw hat and her old-fashioned rubber work boots pushing a wheelbarrow filled with hay.

"Wake up, everyone!," she sang out, after the feeding. "Who wants pancakes with homemade syrup?" By the time we fell out of bed, Diane had breakfast on the table.

"Eat up. I want us to ride to the lake before noon," she cheerfully announced while tossing pancakes onto our plates. By late morning, we had the horses saddled and were riding down the steep rocky grade to Folsom Lake. We crossed streams shaded by oaks, rode through meadows blooming with yellow wildflowers, and raced down to the water's edge where we coaxed our horses into the lake for a well-deserved dip. Back at the ranch, after the exhilarating ride, we unsaddled, brushed our horses, then dove into the pool for a vigorous game of water volley ball.

As the sun dropped behind the hills, Diane offered hors d'oeuvres and drinks. The next thing we knew, Diane, wearing white shorts and a Mexican ruffled blouse was walking down the knoll from her house in high-heeled mule pumps carrying a huge tray filled with food and drinks.

"Diane, let us help," we shouted, as she came seesawing down the hill.

"Oh no, I'm fine, just get the barbecue going," and in the same breath, "how do you like my pumps?" Aunt Buff sent them, Saks Fifth Avenue no less." She raised an eyebrow and laughed.

When night fell, we laid our sleeping bags next to our children's and while looking up at the stars in the black sky we talked and talked and talked. We shared much those warm summer nights with each other and with our children. Men, of course, were a major topic. We talked of the men in our lives and of the men we *wished* were in our lives. All of us, including our daughters, were drawn to the rugged, masculine, "can-do-anything" type of guys. We didn't often meet them.

"Aunt Diane," Christianna piped up, when this subject arose. "Remember when you put an ad in the personal section of the paper and titled it 'redheaded bombshell likes leather and lace?'"

"Yeah," her daughter Kim laughed, "and most of the guys who wrote back were in Vacaville Prison."

Then it was Daniella's turn to embarrass me. "What about mom? Remember that guy Ricardo she dated? But she kept forgetting his name and called him Carlos all the time? And he'd get mad and say, 'The next time you call me Carlos, I'm out of here!'"

Those were easy, lazy summer nights, and in that kind of atmosphere we were relaxed and confident enough to laugh at ourselves.

Since Diane and LouAnn had also shared the experience of divorce, it was natural to talk about the pain of the break-up of our families, how we and our children survived, and, in the end, had all got through it.

"I listen to this love song, all the time, over and over again," LouAnn said. "The words are exactly how I want to love and be loved. I want nothing less—for me and for my children."

"I probably listen to the same love song," Diane interrupted, "and feel the same way. But my main concern for now is keeping my dream—this ranch. Boarding horses, was the best idea I ever came up with."

"I miss being married," I said. Everyone was suddenly quiet. "I do. I'm lonely. I want a man to love, a man to give pleasure to, a soulmate."

These long night discussions helped to heal and empower us. We had our dreams and we were going to shoot for them. As we fell asleep, the stars shone down on our expectant faces.

We've continued these sleep-overs, surrounded by our children, until this day, only our ages and the conversations have changed. But communication and laughter are still the bonds that hold us together.

Trey, too, could always boost my spirits and I was fortunate that he continued to play a part in our lives. In September of 1988 my hope of achieving a more rewarding life were hastened when Trey and I found ourselves involved in another television project with David Zuccolotto, a lovable, big-hearted, gorgeous Italian. He was an ex-minister, counselor and a single parent with a "million dollar" comic strip concept, called *Dr. Sickmund Fred*. When we first met David, he was writing this satire on psychology that was being published in journals and small northern California newspapers. His character, Dr. Sickmund Fred, was a kooky, lovable cartoon psychologist with a unique and witty perspective on life. He shared an office with his outlandish, sometimes troublesome mutt, Pavlov, and his German secretary, Anna.

David came up with the idea of writing a television sitcom blending reality and fantasy titled, *Lenor's Place with Dr. Sickmund Fred.* The sitcom was to be my true story with a magical twist: After the morning paper arrives, Lenor reads her favorite comic strip, "Dr. Sickmund Fred." Suddenly, the characters come alive with animation that only Lenor can see. While the other comic characters maintain their usual form, Dr. Sickmund and Pavlov leap from the strip and land in Lenor's world of problems and misadventures.

With great expectations and a six-page television treatment, David, Trey and I went to LA..With the help of Trey's dad, we set up meetings at NBC, Hanna-Barbera, and Paramount.

We arrived, practically broke. But we pooled our resources, rented a room for a week and set up headquarters. David tells our Park Hotel story best: "We were staying at a pretty nice hotel, considering our circumstances, that a friend arranged for us to get at a discount. It even had a separate bedroom which Lenor called the master suite and of course, occupied. Trey and I had to sleep on the couch and the floor. One morning, we awoke to a tremendous pounding on the door. It was Trey's dad who showed up early to prepare us for a meeting in our hotel with a television executive. Trey, half-naked, struggling to put his pants on, opened the door to a pretty embarrassing scene: clothes everywhere, blankets and pillows scattered in disarray all over the floor; Trey in only his shorts and Lenor hollering from the messy master suite, 'David, where's my leg? Please find my leg, I've got to get dressed!' "

Day after day for two weeks we met with directors, producers, and heads of studios pitching our proposal.

"We love you, Baby. We'll be calling you!" was the response.

But there were no calls.

Once again, Trey and I faced disappointment, and along with David, shared in the pain of rejection. But it only served to strengthen our loving relationship.

"When I think back to when we first met," David recalls, "I think of what a wreck I was, and how you and Trey rescued me when I was falling apart. You guys allowed me to let off steam and listened to my dreams. You accepted my weaknesses and mistakes. And, you always had a way of making our most recent failures sound like opportunities. We'd be sitting around the fireplace with Trey, the girls and little Elliott, talking and laughing, and you, Lenor, would come up with my favorite Madrugaism, 'Remember this moment!' And Daniella would roll her eyes and say 'OOOH, mother!', but we all loved it, and it worked."

After the washout with *Lenor's Place with Dr. Sickmund Fred*, I realized that the success or failure of a venture is not important. What matters is the joy in the process of coming up with an idea and seeing it through, then having the guts to let it go.

After a five month adventure with *Dr. Sickmund Fred*, I was back at Kelly Girls; Trey back to teaching. David continued to write his comic strip and tried to get it nationally syndicated. Though he aroused interest from many newspapers, his comic strip was never picked up by the major newspapers.

On October 16, 1989, at 5:05 P.M. I played my final role at masquerading. I had been on the job as a cashier at the local Cadillac dealership only one week when my boss entered the tiny glass cage were I was struggling to balance accounts. I knew she was there to fire me, but just as she was opening her mouth, the Santa Cruz 7.2 earthquake struck. We heard a huge roar, then a rumble, then the ground began to violently shake. The glass surrounding us crackled and splintered. Nearby, decorative cement Greek statues shook. Heads, arms, torsos and legs began to crumble all over the brand new Cadillacs and onto the showroom floor. I immediately lost my balance and fell to the ground. My boss panicked and tried to flee the building. Too late. With the might of a pit bull, I grabbed her leg and clung to it. She kicked and cursed while trying to free herself of me and the destruction that was falling all around us.

"You'll be safe in the door frame," I yelled, hoping she wouldn't leave me. She didn't, or couldn't, because of my death grip.

We waited out the after-shocks together. Later, she thanked me, and pointing to the exit that was plugged-up with heavy debris, said that I had probably saved her life. Saving her life, however, didn't make her any more sympathetic to my efforts at portraying a cashier. In the end, I lost not only my footing that day, but also my job.

It didn't matter. When I arrived home I got a surprise phone call from my New York agent. "*Reader's Digest* just bought the international world rights to your book," he said.

"What? My book was published over ten years ago," I said surprised. "Is this possible?"

"I have a rather large check to prove it," my agent said.

I thanked my agent and I thanked God that I would no longer need to masquerade.

That summer, with money in the bank, I was able to get back to writing and lecturing. Christianna, who had graduated from Cabrillo Junior College and was preparing to enter San Diego State, got a job at Harbor Hills mental hospital as a psychiatric nurse's assistant. She was thrilled with this opportunity, as she planned to major in psychology. Christianna loved her patients, and they loved her because she had a unique understanding of their individual problems. Afternoons, she would get permission to take a few of her patients on long walks down to the beach or to the corner grocery store where they could buy candy and cigarettes. Friday nights were Disco Nights at Harbor Hills. Christianna would arrange these dances, and the patients enjoyed them so much that if they were to be released on Friday, they would request an extra day's stay so they wouldn't miss out on the much anticipated dance.

Daniella completed her junior year at the alternative school by skipping one grade. It was about this time that Daniella came home from the beach one afternoon with a new girlfriend.

"You ought to meet my dad," Pam said to me.

"Yeah?" I asked. "Does he wear cowboy boots?"

"Yes, and he flies his own plane."

"Well, tell him to come on over!" I laughed.

My life was about to make a dramatic change.

Chapter 8
Blue Skies

"Roy *walks* for me, I *hear* for him."

In my bedroom, I was struggling to shove my rigid, dummy foot into its shoe when I heard Pam's father, Roy, knock at the door. I yelled for him to come up. After I finally got my shoe on, I touched up my lipstick, checked one last time that my dress wasn't hung up on my brace and swung open the bedroom door. In the living room I found Roy browsing through my bookcase.

I didn't expect my blind date to be quite so handsome or tall. His coarse, dark hair, was parted to the side and swung freely, giving him a disheveled "little boy" look. He wore a wrinkled western shirt, jeans, and a belt with an airplane insignia on the buckle. He was even wearing cowboy boots. I liked what I saw.

Startled to see me *walk* into the room, he said, hesitating, "I'm sorry for staring, but I thought you'd be in a wheelchair."

Far from being offended, I was impressed by his forthrightness. I told him it was okay, that most people thought the same thing before meeting me.

As I poured some wine for us, Roy eagerly moved about the apartment, curious and asking questions. "How do you get up these stairs?" he asked, looking down the steep staircase that he'd just climbed that led up to the apartment I now rented. "Block and tackle?" He raised an eyebrow and laughed.

I enjoyed his humor and the cheeky anticipation written all over his face. And he had a smile that made me want to smile back.

But when we drove off to dinner in a huge, *la bamba*, 1972 Oldsmobile Royale, with a vinyl, two-tone, pea-green-and-white interior, I had second thoughts.

Roy tapped the plastic dashboard. "How do you like the car?"

"Oh, it's beautiful," I said, rolling my eyes.

But cars don't say everything about a man, so as we drove on, I asked, "What do you do for a living?"

"I fix TV's," he said.

"Ah, great," I said, forcing a smile. "Where do you live?"

"With my mom in Watsonville."

"Oh, charming," I said, swallowing my smile. All of what I was hearing didn't seem too promising, but I was leaving things open.

We ate dinner at the Deer Park Inn, a rustic, old Santa Cruz hang-out where game trophies hang from knotty pine walls, and sat at a cozy table for two. One small candle illuminated Roy's soft blue eyes from across the table. He was warm and attentive, and his easy smile drew me in.

We lingered for a long time at that table, getting acquainted. Roy was interested in my years as a farm wife, how I had lost my leg, my life as an author and what I'd been doing since my divorce. I was interested in Roy's past, as well. He told me he had three daughters from his first marriage who were now grown and living on their own. He mentioned that he'd been working for over twenty years with his best friend, George, who owned a television and satellite shop. "George has been like a father to me," Roy said. "He taught me to fly airplanes back in 1968. He brought me into his business, too. I owe him a lot."

When Roy described his love of motorcycles and the road trips he often took on his Honda 550 across the deserts of California and Nevada, I began to sense a free spirit and little bit of rebel in him. "I just love to hop on that motorcycle and hit the road, not knowing where I'll bed down. No reservations for me, " he laughed.

I liked the feeling of independence he expressed—right up my alley.

As we continued to talk, I noticed that he mispronounced certain words. Knowing it wasn't ignorance, I blurted out, "How come you talk funny?"

"I do?" he responded, acting surprised. Then he laughed. "No, no, I'm kidding," he said, touching my hand. "I was born with fifty percent hearing loss in one ear and seventy in the other. But I get along okay. I partly read people's lips, and then I rely on their body language."

When I pressed Roy for more details, he told me that when he was a kid, he always thought that what he heard was normal, until he entered the first grade. "The older kids used to make fun of me," Roy told me, leaning across the table. "I couldn't hear them, but I knew by their body language that they were talking about me. They'd point and yell, 'There's the deaf and dumb boy!'"

Sensing my sympathy and interest, Roy went on.

"I always made a point of sitting in the back of the class so the teachers wouldn't notice me and ask questions I couldn't hear. One day, the teacher asked me to stand up and read aloud. My heart sank because I knew I couldn't pronounce the words correctly.

"'We're waiting,' my teacher said. 'Please begin.' But before I had finished the first sentence, the kids were laughing. My teacher told me to pronounce the words as they were written. 'Can't you read the book?' she asked. I was so embarrassed! I told her I could *read* the book, but I couldn't *hear* the book."

There was that sense of humor again. Only this time, I sensed, he was making light of the pain of ridicule he had suffered as a child, and it touched a place in my heart.

It was late by the time we left the restaurant, but I wasn't ready for this very special evening to end, so when Roy asked if I wanted to go out to the local airport, I readily agreed.

When we arrived, I was impressed to see him open the gate with a card. He drove up to a string of hangars, jumped out of the car, rolled opened a heavy hangar door, and switched on the lights. I gasped at what I saw before me: a plane from a different time and place, and under each wing sat a Corvette.

Roy patted the engine cowling of the plane. "It's a classic, 1946 Super Cruiser PA-12 tail dragger," he said, proudly. " It's the type of plane bush pilots use in Alaska, a standard STOL—good for Short Take-Offs and Landings. It's a faithful old bird. I've flown it across America—all the way from here to Rockland Owls Head, on the coast of Maine and back."

"Wow! Where did you get it?" I asked, even more intrigued.

He told me he had found it in bits and pieces in a neighbor's garage back in 1972. The wings and fuselage were the only parts that weren't dismantled. He bought it on the spot for $2,500.00.

"I really got excited when I saw it," he said. "It was just like the balsa model plane my dad brought home for me when I was twelve years old. I'd been in bed for over a year with rheumatic fever, so my folks tried to keep my mind occupied with things to do, like putting the model plane together. I painted it yellow, like the Super Cub on the box. My dad hung it over my bed where I could lie back and let my imagination soar like the plane. I was in the cockpit, out of my bed, and flying off to far-away places," he said, with a wide grin. Then he bounded to the side of the plane, telling more about the Cruiser. "It's a *can do* airplane," he said, "like a jeep, you might say, in the aviation field."

My attention, however, was on the cars sitting under the wings of the plane.

"Are these your Corvettes?" I asked.

"Yah," he said, walking over to the aqua one that looked like it just came off a showroom floor. "This one's a '59 and that one is a 1980."

"Well," I said, hesitating, but dying to know, "why didn't you pick me up in one of those?"

"I thought you'd be more comfortable in my mother's Olds, " Roy said, matter-of-factly.

When Roy dropped me off that night, I was floating. What a guy, I thought. So considerate and kind. And I liked the way he underplayed the material things he had, like the plane and Corvettes. I climbed into bed and drifted into sleep thinking how refreshing it was to be with such a man. He made all the other men I'd dated since leaving the farm seem inconsequential.

"Well, Mom, what did you think of Roy?" the girls asked the next morning.

"He's handicapped," I joked. "He can't hear, and he pronounces his words funny."

"MOTHER!" They yelled.

That night I anxiously waited for Roy to call. When the phone finally rang, I tried to remain calm and not sound too excited.

"Do you want to do a little night flying?" he asked, brief and to the point.

"Night flying?" I gulped.

Before this, prior to even considering getting on a private plane, I'd need a stiff drink. But, I thought, if I wanted to get to know this man better, I would have to bite the bullet and try to overcome my fear.

"I'd love to," I said.

"Meet me at the airport in an hour, and bring a jacket. It might get a little breezy up there."

"Breezy?"

My heart racing, I drove to the airport. I was excited but scared, too, thinking about flying at night. What if we crashed? And what if I got trapped in the plane because I couldn't get out on my own? I was putting a lot of trust in this man I'd only just met.

"Hi there," Roy said, with that winning smile of his, as I got out of my car. "I've already done the pre-flight check. We're ready to go. We fly tandem, so you'll have to sit in the back seat. Jump in."

Jump in? "How?" I asked. "There are no steps."

"Just hop in backwards. Push your body lightly against the wing strut, and then lift yourself up on to the seat with your hands."

Wing strut? I thought, as I tried to follow his directions.

"Now, use the post for support, and slide in," he said, as he gently guided me, "and see if you can get in the rest of the way on your own."

I did okay. I got in. I usually prefer doing these kinds of things on my own, but this time I caught myself thinking how nice it would be to have Roy's muscular arms lifting me into the plane.

We took off over the ocean, made a wide turn above Santa Cruz and then flew atop the Loma Prieta mountains that separate Monterey Bay and the Santa Clara Valley. From one side of the mountains I could see the shimmering lights of San Francisco and San Jose and from the other side Salinas, Monterey and Moss Landing. My anxiety about flying eased when Roy began to explain the mechanics of the plane and other unknowns like turbulence, updrafts, down drafts and wind. Soon, I was so absorbed in the thrill of flying with this man in his small plane at night, that I completely forgot my fear and was able to enjoy our short flight over the mountains and back to Watsonville airport.

Roy and I began seeing each other on a regular basis after that first night flight. And with Roy, the mandate for a date was adventure. We took road trips in his '59 Corvette or motorcycled along the winding, cliff-hanging, coastal Highway One to Big Sur; we made spontaneous flights to quaint towns like Carmel Valley or Half Moon Bay for breakfast or lunch, and he took me along when he competed in classic car and air show events.

The turning point in our relationship began one evening as when we were parked on the cliffs of Santa Cruz overlooking the harbor lights, sipping champagne and kissing madly like two crazy teenagers. Then we went to my apartment.

"Would you like to come in?" I asked, as Roy escorted me up the stairs to my door.

"I'd like that," he said, giving me a friendly kiss on the forehead.

"Why don't you get a fire going, and I'll just slip into something more comfortable," I said.

Excited, not at all worried, as I had been with Didder so many years earlier, I took off my leg and slipped into a black negligee. Roy was lying in front of the fireplace when I crutched into the room. He didn't say a word, just smiled shyly as I turned on some romantic French music and then lay down beside him.

"How do you like the music?" I asked.

"Oh, I like it," he said, acting like he could hear it.

"Would you like to dance?" I asked.

"Dance?" he said, surprised.

But when I stood up, balancing myself on one leg, he followed, drawing me into his arms. I placed my right foot on the top of his left foot, and we danced. We danced to the music of *Les Modernes*, and we danced and danced…right into my bedroom.

Without modesty or any inhibitions, we made love, as if we belonged together. It felt like I'd come home. Truly home…*and love slowly moved in.*

The next morning, Roy awakened me with a kiss. "Do you like to camp?" he asked, out of nowhere.

"Camp? I love to camp, " I said, even though I'd never camped in my life. It didn't matter, I just wanted to be with him. If it meant camping, flying or going to the moon.

Roy explained that there would be a fly-in that week-end of pilots who owned tail dragger planes at Georgetown Airport in the Sierras. He suggested we go and camp on the runway. "If we take off soon," he said with growing excitement, "we'll have time to land on some of the airstrips in the Sierras that I've never landed on before."

"The Sierra Mountains? Strips you've never landed on before? Oookay…"

I didn't have much time to think further on the matter, because once we got to the airport and Roy had pulled the Cruiser out of the hangar and had done his pre-flight check, we were off, flying north over the mountains, across the vast San Joaquin Valley and into the Sierras.

From the back seat, Roy's head, neck and shoulders were only inches from my touch. I looked at his rugged, confident profile. His aviation glasses were shining as they caught the sun's rays. For a moment, heat rose to my face as I remembered the passion we had shared only last night. This man literally took my breath away.

As we approached the Sierras and the first dirt strip Roy was aiming for, I got a little nervous when I could barely see it from the air. When I asked Roy if it was safe, he told me not to worry, that it was fine, but that mountain flying can be deceptive. "Mountains can appear to be either climbing or descending," he said, over the engine's roar, "depending on how you approach them. If you've been flying for a long time, you might think the strip is higher than it should be. It's only an optical illusion, but it leaves little room for mistakes on landings or take-offs."

I pulled my seatbelt in a little tighter, but Roy made a perfect landing there at Alta Sierra Airport where Chuck Yeager, the World War II fighting ace and first man to fly faster than the speed of sound, lived at that time. We then flew to Brownsville and headed toward the Feather River Canyon where we encountered billowy, cotton shaped, cumulus clouds. As Roy flew gracefully over and around them, it felt like we were flying through Elysian fields.

Before getting to the canyon, I spotted Lake Orville below, where my family used to spend summer vacations. We approached the Feather River Canyon and flew below its rim. Boxed between clay-colored canyon walls, we followed the winding, serpentine river. As we flew, I could see a freight train clinging to the mountainside, its engine and mix-matched cars snaking in and out of dark holes that penetrated deep into the craggy mountains. After the dramatic flight through the canyon, we cleared the ridge and headed for Quincy airport in the north mid-range of the Sierras.

We had hoped to eat lunch at the airport cafe when we arrived, but it was closed.

"Let's walk into town," Roy said. "It's only a half-mile."

I was willing, but realistically, I was uncertain that I could make it. A mile round trip is a long way for me to walk.

But Roy, it seemed, could make all things possible. He lent me his strong arm for support and kicked away the brush and rocks that blocked my path as we walked. Once when I stumbled, Roy caught me just in time. He looked down and saw that the shoe lace on my dummy foot had come loose. He crouched down on his knees and tied my shoe. A profound tenderness swept over me, to see this big man, the muscles of his back and shoulders straining against the seams of his shirt, gently taking care of my needs. I'd been looking after myself for such a long time, I'd almost forgotten how good it felt to be looked after again.

We had a quick lunch in town and a long walk back to the airport. We flew the next leg of our journey to Truckee-Tahoe airport. At an altitude of 10,000 feet, I couldn't help but feel vulnerable, especially since our only protection from the earth below was Roy's small, single-engine, fabric-covered airplane. "It's like a five-cent rag blowing in the wind," he laughed.

But Roy must have sensed my panic because he reached back and grabbed my ankle (the wrong one) and said, "Do you know what a privilege it is to be up here, flying? Look around you. How many people get this opportunity?"

Roy was right, and my uneasiness began to dissipate. *Privilege* was the key word, and it opened up a whole new world for me. For the first time, I no longer felt earth bound. I let my spirit soar with the plane. My physical body ascended, too, unencumbered by boundaries, freed from being confined, unbalanced and slowed down. I wasn't having to orchestrate every move, every step. I felt normal. God, what a blessing it was to be free, if just for a while, from my disability. I felt a deep gratitude to this man who had given me such a gift.

The raw excitement of flying tandem, over vast terrain with unparalleled vistas, only added to my new infatuation with flying. From one side of the plane, I could see the surreal arid Nevada desert, and on the other side, the contrasting verdant Sierra Mountains. A privilege, indeed.

Over Truckee airport, Roy had to use a slip maneuver to land because of heavy cross-winds. The Cruiser didn't have flaps like standard planes, so to lose altitude without building up air speed, Roy had to cross control the ailerons and rudders. He banked the left wing down toward the runway and slipped it in sideways against the cross-winds. He then straightened out the plane just before we touched down.

After I caught my breath, Roy took off again and we flew over Donner Lake, and on to Blue Canyon. Finally, we headed toward Georgetown where we planned to camp at the fly-in. Although there had been a number of times when a difficult take-off or landing or a sudden banking of the plane due to turbulence caused me, in Beryl Markham's words, "to contemplate my small courage," I learned to trust Roy that day. I knew I was in good hands.

When we flew over Georgetown, I could see the airstrip atop a plateau overlooking the American River Canyon on one end, and trees and hills on the other side. It looked like an "airport in the sky" to me.

Roy landed on our first approach. He tied down the plane alongside the runway and set up a pup tent underneath the wing. From a storage compartment in the back of the plane came a small barbecue, two steaks, a can of hot chili beans, flour tortillas and a bottle of red wine.

So this was camping…

Roy asked if I'd be comfortable sleeping in the tent.

"Oh, yes, of course," I said. It wasn't exactly true, but I wasn't about to tell Roy it might be uncomfortable for me to sleep on the ground. "But, where can I put my leg?" I asked.

Roy flung my leg, still clad in blue jeans and white sock and tennis shoe, over his shoulder and placed it in the cock-pit of the Cruiser, heel to sky. Throughout the evening, pilots had to pass by our plane to get to the hangar festivities. Come morning, we overheard two pilots laughing. "My God," one said to the other, "does that woman ever have stamina!"

After spending the morning admiring the many classic tail draggers that lined the runway, Roy and I hitch-hiked two miles into Georgetown. The moment we stepped onto the worn plank walkways, we fell in love with the historic little gold-mining town. We walked around, admiring the typical western front stores, stopping at little saddlers' shops and Indian crafts stores. Finally, thoroughly charmed, we found ourselves in front of the old Georgetown Hotel. Once inside, we sat in front of a rock fireplace with a slow- burning fire and ate a hearty meal of buffalo stew.

After lunch, while enjoying hot mugs of spicy apple cider, we noticed a cow bell dangling from the ceiling. We asked the bartender about it.

"Well, you see," he began with a sly grin, "that bell up there is wired through the ceiling to the bedsprings in that upstairs room. Whenever the bed moves, the bell rings. Some nights, we get a whole lot of clappin' down here," he chuckled.

He also mentioned that the hotel had housed a notorious brothel back in the 1800's. "The original room is still here," he said, " but nobody's allowed up there."

Curious, Roy and I sneaked up the back staircase of the hotel to find it. We did, by way of a ceiling door that led to the attic. Roy opened it, and we inched our way up the narrow stairs and entered a large living area encircled by small, six-by-eight-foot cubicles.

"These tiny rooms must have been where the ladies entertained," I whispered.

"Not much for privacy," Roy laughed.

We wandered about, fascinated to see rusted iron bed frames still in place; spindly, wooden chairs and once sturdy commodes broken and scattered about; and tattered, old- fashioned elongated shades still hanging from attic windows. When we heard voices coming from the floor below, we figured we'd better leave before we got caught. As we crept back down the stairs, I thought what a good sport Roy was, ready for anything. And when I mentioned this to him, he said, "*You're* the good sport."

After this thorough snooping of the Georgetown Hotel, we set out to explore the rest of the town. We stopped in front of a pair of iron fire doors that sealed off a small brick building that looked abandoned. When we peeked in the windows, we saw it was a real estate office. Roy was interested in the pictures hanging on the walls describing property for sale.

An older man opened the door and greeted us. "Come on in," he said and asked what we were looking for, as he walked toward his desk.

I could immediately see he was an amputee, wearing an out-dated wooden leg that looked like more of an encumbrance than an aid. When I mentioned that I, too, was an amputee, and pulled up my pant leg to show him, he said, "That's some leg you got there, gal. I've had this thing for over twenty years. It's too late for me to try to wear a fancy leg like yours. Anyway, I'm used to dragging this old thing around."

I had seen this before in other long-time amputees who hated to think about being fitted with something new that might not work. They continue to wear their original, worn-out prosthesis, which, after years of use, usually doesn't fit properly making walking even more painful.

While I was trying to tell the agent about the advances in prosthetics, Roy interrupted us. "Excuse me," he said, holding a photo in his hand. "It says here that this property is near the airport."

"It sure is," the realtor said. "Five beautiful acres on a hill-top. Would you like to see it?"

Roy said he would, so the realtor drove us up to the site. "I'll wait in the car," he said as he parked below the hill. "It's a little harder for me to get around." He smiled and added with no envy, "But you'll have no problem getting up that hill, not with that new fandangled leg of yours. You're a damn lucky little gal."

"God, Roy," I said, frustrated for the man as we climbed the hill. "How I wish he'd get rid of that old leg. He could be so much more active and comfortable with a new one."

"Why don't you tell him?" Roy said.

"I did, I tried, back at his office, but he didn't want to hear it."

While the realtor waited, Roy and I walked the land. Fallen pine needles crunched underneath our feet. A slight gust of wind stirred the crisp sweet smell of cedar, oak, madrone and manzanita. Suddenly, Roy stopped. Under the canopy of forest, he drew me into his arms and held me there. We were both quiet, content. We stood at the top of the hill looking at the Sierra Mountain range, and for a moment, I dared to envision sharing a life here with Roy.

"So what do you think of the property?" he asked me.

"I love it!" I said.

That afternoon, Roy made an offer on the property. Before he signed, he asked me again, "You're sure you like it?"

"Oh, yes, yes, it's beautiful," I said.

For the first time, I wondered if Roy was including me in his future. Or was I setting myself up for disappointment? But that night back at the airport, sleeping in the tent, enfolded in Roy's arms, I knew there was a chance at love and, maybe, permanence.

Five months after we met, Roy moved in with me. It had been eight years since I'd lived with a man. A long time. Time enough to miss a man's presence: his shirts hanging from the closet with his boots tumbled below, the sound of his heavy belt buckle hitting the floor before he slips into bed. Now, I could enjoy the anticipation of my man coming home from work, as I prepared a fine dinner, chilled a bottle of wine and lit up the logs in the fireplace to create just the right atmosphere. I was grateful to have and to give these pleasures once again.

Before we lived together, Roy had never seen me put on my leg. I always made sure I dressed before or after he did. I wasn't ashamed of my body, but I was self-conscious about the bulky contraption I had to put on each day. Strapping on a leg is nothing like slipping on a pair of sexy panties. But, one morning, Roy woke up while I was in the process of putting on my leg. Sleepy, he turned over on his back, put his arms behind his head, smiled up at me and watched.

"I know, it's not a pretty sight," I said, embarrassed as I awkwardly turned away from his stare.

"Oh, no, I think it's incredible," he said, jumping out of bed. "Can I look at it?" He bent down and probed the ankle, knee and thigh with his hand. "What a gadget. My god, it's magnificent."

I should have known that Roy would have been interested in my leg. The mechanics of it captivated him. And from that day on, he's carried a small screwdriver in the pocket of his shirt wherever we go. "Just in case your leg ever has a screw loose," he says.

Christianna was in her second year at San Diego State University and Daniella was finishing her senior year at high school, when Roy moved in.

Daniella liked Roy the moment she met him. It took Christianna a little longer. She still held hope that her dad and I would get back together. But, Christianna, too, fell under Roy's charms, after a midnight flight to my sister's wedding in Auburn, California.

I had driven up to Diane's the day before to help with preparations. Christianna, home from college that summer and working part-time in a mental hospital, couldn't get off work until around 11 P.M. Earlier, Roy had offered to fly her to the wedding. I said it wasn't necessary because she wouldn't be getting off work until late, and could catch a ride with one of our friends the next day.

"Oh, no," Roy said. "I promised I'd fly her over, and I will. It doesn't matter how late. I'll wait."

Once again, he showed his considerate ways, and my love grew deeper.

By the time they took off that misty night, fog had rolled in and covered the runway at Watsonville airport. But, Roy found an opening in the fog and flew out fast. Once over the mountains, he knew it would be clear to Auburn, which is located in the foothills of the Sierras.

Later, Christianna said she felt like she was a character in the final scene of *Casablanca*, where the pilot takes off in the fog in the dark of night.

When Diane and I got to Auburn airport to pick up Roy and Christianna, we were a little concerned that the runway lights were not on. We didn't know then that Roy could activate the lights from the control stick of his Cruiser. He clicked it seven times, and within five seconds—bam! the entire runway lit up.

I was leaning on my crutches at the end of the runway ramp, wearing a long, flowing white negligee and waving a bottle of champagne.

"My god, I hope that's not my mom!'" Christianna yelled.

"My god, I hope it is," Roy yelled back.

My sister got married the next afternoon at her favorite place in all the world, her horse ranch in the foothills near Folsom Lake. As Diane and her groom, Gordon, exchanged vows under an ancient oak tree, I wondered who would be next? I prayed it would be me.

It was only a few months later, as I lay on the bed reading and waiting for Roy to get off work so we could fly to a "Moon Night Fly-In" down in Porterville, California, Roy came rushing through the door and jumped onto the bed beside me.

"I have something *very* important to discuss with you," he said, solemnly.

I got scared thinking that maybe something was wrong, and maybe it had to do with us. (After Joseph's surprise betrayal so many years ago, it was still hard for me to take anything for granted.)

"Will you marry me?" Roy asked with a big grin, as he pulled a ring from his shirt pocket dangling from his little screw driver.

I started crying. And I couldn't stop crying. It took me about three minutes to compose myself enough to give Roy an answer. "Yes, yes, oh, yes, I'll marry you."

My prayers were answered.

On March 9th, 1991, Roy's forty-eighth birthday, we were married in the American River Inn Hotel in Georgetown. My daughters were my proud bridesmaids. After the small ceremony with a few family and friends in attendance, we all marched down Main Street to the Georgetown Hotel. We swung open the saloon doors to the sounds of honky-tonk music being played by local musicians, and began to celebrate through the night with loggers, barmaids, bikers and other townspeople.

The next morning, when Roy and I came downstairs, our friends were already in the bar drinking Bloody Mary's. They cheered as we entered.

"Hey, we've been here since last night," they teased. "Couldn't get no sleep, not with that old cow bell ringing all night long!" I laughed, but Roy's face turned an almighty red.

We lived in Santa Cruz during the first six months of our marriage. Most week-ends we flew to Georgetown where we stayed on our property in a 12'x 8' trailer. If we were home, we'd often hang out with Roy's pilot friends at the airport. "The pilot lounge is where we do our best flying," Roy would joke.

One of Roy's friends, Hans, a handsome thirty-seven-year-old engineer from Norway, made a lasting impression on me. A few years back, he had crashed his glider in the Sierras. For three days and nights he lay in the wreckage in freezing temperatures, conscious but unable to move. He was located by a search and rescue team and rushed to a hospital where he was told the horrific news that both of his legs had to be amputated below the knees, and that he was paralyzed from the waist down. Doctors said that his flying days were over.

Though Hans accepted his physical losses, he wasn't going to accept the idea of never flying again. After two years in recovery and extensive rehabilitation, he bought a Grob109 motorized glider. He re-rigged it so he could control the rudders with his hands instead of his legs, and he was flying again.

The day I met him, we talked for a long time, sharing our stories and discussing phantom limb pain. "The only time I'm free from constant, physical pain," Hans said, rubbing his stumps, "is when I'm in the glider searching for that perfect, mean black cloud that can give me the lift I need to turn off the motor and glide." He was quiet for a moment.

Abruptly, he asked if I would like to go up and "fly around the pattern." I agreed readily, though inwardly I was a little uneasy.

"I'm jealous," Roy teased, as he walked me out to the glider. "You're getting the chance to fly in a Grob." I knew he was deliberately trying to shift my concern about flying with a paralyzed, double amputee pilot.

Hans rolled out to the glider in his wheelchair. He backed to the edge of the wing, hoisted himself into a sitting position and lifted the chair onto his lap. He released each wheel and placed it behind the pilot's seat of the two-place glider. He folded the wheel-chair on top and then raised himself up and slid inside the cockpit. I, on the other hand, had to struggle to get into the plane with my artificial leg. I could never have managed, if Roy hadn't vigorously pushed and shoved, until I was finally in the glider next to Hans.

Before we took off, I nudged Hans. "Do you realize," I said with a wink, "that between the two of us, we're on our last leg?"

During that first year of marriage with Roy, I had never been happier. My heart was full of love for my husband. I found, as we grew more intimate, that I had not only a partner in laughter, passion and adventure, but also a strong supporter of my work.

A short time after we were married, I had a speaking engagement at Hospice, an organization that cares for the terminally ill. I suggested that Roy didn't need to come and hear me talk, since he'd heard me before, but he assured me he wanted to be there. "I always hear something new," he said.

Roy flew me to the Hospice engagement and personally greeted everyone at the door. "Don't you look nice?" he said, sincerely. "I'm so happy you've come to hear my wife speak. Please sit down. Can I get you anything?"

As I saw my husband's attention and concern for the patients and their care-givers, I thought, once again, how dear this man was to me. It was then that I realized that Roy's understanding of the needs of others came from the fact that he, too, lives with a handicap.

But Roy doesn't think he's limited. Quite the opposite. He feels that because of his loss of hearing, he has been forced to discover and understand, on his own, things that interest him—the universe, geology, chemistry, electricity, satellite communication, aviation, anything mechanical and on and on. One of our running jokes is the time I was relaxing by the fire reading Anais Nin and asked Roy what he was reading.

"Parts," he said.

Roy also believes that his affliction has enabled him to develop a special sense for flying. He usually knows exactly what's going on mechanically with the plane, not so much by sound, but by the vibrations from the stick or from the engine itself. "When I fly," he says, "it's like the plane and I are one."

We had been married for seven months when Roy burst through the door brimming with excitement. "Honey, let's move to Georgetown."

"Well, it sounds wonderful but…"

"I've figured it out," he said. "If I sell off the property and stocks and bonds I've accumulated over the years, we'll be able to move and maybe build our dream house—a log home. Well, honey, what do you think?"

Of course, I loved the idea. We already enjoyed spending week-ends in Georgetown, so we knew it was a place we could live. But after Roy checked out the particulars of building there and discovered it would be very expensive, we decided to look for land in southern Oregon. Later, we decided we could build a small get-away cabin in Georgetown.

In Roy's Cruiser, we scouted out Oregon. We were enchanted by the mountains, trees, open spaces, rivers and lakes. Whenever we saw property from the air that caught our eye, we'd land at the nearest airstrip, call up a realtor and ask to be shown around. After a few trips, we decided to settle in Evans Valley, a beautiful wooded area twelve miles from the Rogue River and about sixty miles north of the California border.

We bought a rustic, three-story house on thirty acres, cradled between 4,000 foot mountains and teeming with deer and elk. It had a natural forest, a year-round creek and a pond. We moved into our house in late fall.

When my friends first heard of our move, they were dumbfounded. "You'll be bored to death up there in Oregon," they told me. *Au contraire.*

Since my amputation and brush with death so many years ago, I'm never bored—only exceedingly grateful for every moment of my life.

Roy and I, too, feel blessed to be able to live in the middle of a vast forest with not a house or light in sight. And for the first time in many years, I feel content and secure waking up on autumn mornings with the changing colors of trees and mountains framing every window and Roy firing up the wood-burning stove, luring me downstairs with the smell of freshly-brewed coffee.

After living in Oregon for seven years, Roy and I continue to appreciate not only the land, but the freedom we have. There are no more "masquerades" for me and no more "fixing TV's" for Roy. Instead, he's "fixing-up" and managing the rentals and properties we've been able to acquire over the past few years—not to mention his daily labor of clearing and tending our thirty acres.

My day usually begins with writing. Later, I can hop on my 250 Polaris all-terrain vehicle (ATV) or, as Roy calls it, "my wheelchair," and head for the woods. What independence I feel riding through the forest, taking in its syrupy pine smell, as I wind between the trees. In summer, my destination is always the pond, where I go for a swim with the frogs, fish, wood ducks and other little creatures. In winter, Roy and I enjoy riding our ATV'S in the new-fallen snow and go to the creek where we sit overlooking its rushing current. With snowflakes lightly falling, we talk of our never-ending hopes and dreams. In early spring, we head up the logging roads to the top of the highest mountain for a picnic. We open a bottle of wine, and, inspired by the view of the snow-capped Cascade Mountains and our house below, we toast each other: "To another boring day in Oregon!"

Life is good and full. I continue to feel that I'm in the throes of an enormous love affair. When friends call and ask how things are going, I say what I've said since the beginning: "I'm so in love, I can't think straight."

Epilogue

I write these final words to my manuscript in the early evening of November 26, 1998, sitting on the verandah at the American River Inn in Georgetown, California, where Roy and I were married. It was here we began our journey together that led us from this California gold mining town to our home in Oregon.

Roy continues to fly and restore airplanes. Aside from overhauling the Cruiser, he recently restored a 1963 Cessna 172 and is teaching me to fly. I've logged over twenty hours of flying time so far. I have only one problem: one foot to control two rudders. Once landed, to steer the plane, I must quickly switch my right foot to the left rudder and then back to the right rudder causing the plane to weave down the runway. Pilots in the lounge, look out the window in alarm. "My God, that pilot must be drunk!" And then when I park the plane and get out and walk—"My God, that pilot *is* drunk."

Roy and I also live part of the year in Costa Rica in a small village on the Pacific Coast. In San Jose, the capital city, I work with cancer patients and amputees. I'm involved in trying to get North American prosthetists to volunteer their services in this third world country that is in desperate need of prosthetic expertise.

My daughters have married and live near us in Oregon. The many years I hauled them around to hospitals and rehabilitation centers apparently rubbed off, as, today, they work with individuals who are disabled and mentally challenged. Daniella is a case worker at the County Mental Health Department with over ninety geriatric clients. She married her first love, Elliott, and they recently bought a restaurant in Grants Pass which has become a family affair. Elliott is the master chef, Daniella does the books, Christianna works as a bus-girl on week-ends, her husband, Eddie, helps out as a prep cook and Roy washes dishes on Thursdays. I've volunteered to hostess, but Daniella laughs. "No, mom, we don't want you falling onto everyone's plate."

Christianna works at Rogue Valley Medical Center in the psychiatric ward. She was married three years ago here on our property to Eddie Poling, a native Oregonian, whom she met while they were both working at the medical center. Coincidentally, Christianna was filling a position that Eddie's mom had held for over twenty years—before she was diagnosed with cancer. Sadly, Mrs. Poling passed away shortly after Christianna and Eddie met. Eddie is a paramedic, a fireman, a search and rescue volunteer, and a medic in the Army National Guard. We lovingly call him our G.I. Joe.

Through the years the girls' father, Joseph, has remained close to each of them. And for this, I'm grateful.

Nick, my mentor, and I have remained very close. Multiple sclerosis, unfortunately, has taken its toll and he can no longer stand on his own. But he still gets around on a spiffy, candy apple red electric cart. His destination…usually the gym. Nick's great mind and glorious spirit are with him still. When I asked him recently how he keeps such a positive outlook, he laughed and said, "Misfortune can bite me in the ass, but I'll bite it back."

Greg Stearns, my one-time surrogate son, is married with two children and is a doctor at Kaiser Medical Center in San Diego.

Vivienne Lundquist, the persistent lady who ignored the fact that I was missing a leg and encouraged me to ride again, recently died of a cancerous brain tumor.

Judy Graves, my old roommate, has been diagnosed with cancer a second time. Only this time it's cancer of the stomach. Two years ago, doctors gave her three months to live. Judy, however, has out-lived their prediction and is thriving today. The only thing that gets her down are the monthly chemotherapy treatments that leave her greatly fatigued. "But," she recently told me, "when I'm feeling well, I'm doing everything I always wanted to do—but never got around to doing. I intend to enjoy, and live life to its fullest until…"

Judy, my courageous friend, lost her battle to cancer January 9, 2000 at 11 P.M.

Trey, my dear friend and producer of our television venture, is a high school principal and continues to free-lance at writing and producing television shows. David, my other male friend and cohort in writing our television sitcom, continues to write, and has recently been named the head of a rehabilitation center for troubled teenagers.

Besides Nick, I have another hero: my prosthetist, Carlos Sambrano. I met Carlos when he was only sixteen years old and working with my original prosthetist, Fred Karg, who was the master innovator for hip-disarticulation and hemi-pelvectomy patients. After Fred retired, Carlos advanced prosthetics to an even higher level by utilizing the latest technology and components. For the past twenty years, Carlos has taken pride in keeping me on my feet and walking with a life-like leg that is half the weight of my original prosthesis. Carlos says it's vital that I have a light-weight prosthesis because, unlike below-knee or above-knee amputees who use their stumps to propel their artificial legs, I must use my torso to thrust my leg forward, using twice the energy of a normal amputee. In the past, hip and hemi amputees almost never used an artificial leg, because of the excessive weight and rigidity of the leg.

When I first became an amputee, my prosthesis was an inner-skeletal system with a hard, heavy plastic socket. The foot was made of wood and rubber. Today, the steel parts of my original leg have been replaced by a soft flexible socket and lighter carbon plates and titanium components.

The skeletal system is covered with foam, shaped and covered with a rubberized skin that is tinted to match the exact color of my right leg—I can have a deep tan all year round, if I desire.

More radical amputees are walking today because of advanced technology and the compassionate understanding of prosthetists like Carlos. He says that if we're able to design prosthetics for below-knee and above-knee patients that enable them to run and break records in the paraolympics, we should at least be able to get a hip or hemi patient up and walking and living a normal, active life.

Too often, radical amputees are told that they'll never walk again. Staci is one such patient. Last year, she called me from Kansas, saying that she was going in for a hemi-pelvectomy surgery. She wasn't scared of the cancer or of the surgery. What frightened her was doctors' prognosis that she would never walk again. "I'm only twenty years old," Staci said to me.

"That's what doctors told me twenty-two years ago," I told Staci. "And I've not only been walking all these years, but dancing, riding horses, driving and taking care of the needs of my family.

Today, Staci walks. She called me again recently and said that six months after her successful surgery, she fulfilled her dream to dance with her father at her sister's June wedding.

For the future amputee, Carlos says is that after an amputation, doctors may be able to attach a prosthetic device to the patient's anatomy. Doctors would use some kind of implant that would connect to the remainder of the bone to help secure the prosthetic limb to the body.

Prosthetics, Carlos also says, are becoming more sophisticated with computerized types of limbs that can think for the patient. Computers can tell an artificial leg when to bend, when to speed up and when to slow down. He's hoping to see *Terminator Man* robotics in his lifetime. But the most important thing prosthetists can do today for their patients, Carlos tells me, is to encourage them to walk and then rejoice in their effort.

Carlos is only one of many people whose support and friendship enrich my life. I, in turn, am grateful for every opportunity I have to mentor others facing amputation or disease. My web site receives an average of 1000 hits a month, many from cancer patients or amputees reaching out for advice, courage, and reassurance. I try to help them find the will to restore their lives, too. Today, I continue to write, lecture and volunteer at hospitals and rehabilitation facilities—remembering my promessa and finding enjoyment in fulfilling it.

Women friends have also been a major source of sustenance in my life. Two years ago, I met three talented writers, Melinda Haldeman, Amy Belkin and Diana Coogle, with whom I formed a salon of published writers. This book has been written because of this group support and one motivating word: responsibility.

"You owe it to the public," Amy said to me. "It's your mission, your personal goal to help people. Many who have overcome a major life trauma may think they have paid their dues and not be prepared for the ordinary ups and downs of life. You need to show them how you focused on your goals, instead of your misfortunes. You have a responsibility to help others. You have to do it for them. They are out there waiting. Now, get to work!"

I *did* get to work, and after a year of writing, I took the first seven chapters of this manuscript to a writer's conference in Portland, Oregon to pitch it to agents and publishers. After getting a positive response from many agents at the conference, I called Roy with my good news and to let him know that I'd be home about 2 P.M. that afternoon. Just as I was driving over Sexton Pass near our home, Amy who was with me, noticed a small plane flying above us.

"That pilot might be in trouble," I said, "he's flying too low. There's no airport in these mountains." Just as we crested the mountain top, at about 2000 feet, we saw a Super Cruiser flying at eye level. The pilot was rocking his wings.

"My God, it's Roy!" I screamed, laughing and waving.

"He's escorting you home," Amy said. "How romantic."

And he did, flying alongside us, down the pass, to our local airport.

"This would be a good ending to my book," I said.

"It's not an *ending*," Amy said. "It's a *beginning*."

"I fall, I stand still…I trudge on, I gain a little…
I get more eager and climb higher
and began to see the widening horizon.
Every struggle is a victory."

Helen Keller